Fundamentals of English Grammar

Fundamentals of English Grammar

N.C. Sinha

Published by

PRABHAT PRAKASHAN PVT. LTD.
4/19 Asaf Ali Road,
New Delhi-110002 (INDIA)
e-mail: prabhatbooks@gmail.com

ISBN 978-93-5048-198-1

FUNDAMENTALS OF ENGLISH GRAMMAR
by N.C. Sinha

Price
₹ 450.00 (Rupees Four Hundred Fifty Only)

Printed at
SS Japan Arts, Delhi

"Dedicated to wife Anjali
and
sons Akash & Abhas
for constantly egging me on."

Preface

'Grammar is a repository of rules, governing how words are put together into sentences. These rules govern most constructions in a given language. Grammar is the science of correct use of language. It is concerned only with correct speaking and writing.' Fundamentals of grammar need to be fully comprehended to acquire skills of quality English. English enjoys the status of the World Language. No other language has ever scaled this height. It is the language that encompasses everything in the world. It is used and cherished by millions whose mother tongue is not English. Spoken English, as a natural corollary to that, has become an important tool in our hands today. Without mastery over it, the gateway to success will remain a distant dream in today's globalised market. Need of the hour is to think and act globall. So, the aim of this book is a practical one: an aid to good English, to take you places on the wings of English. The book is designed to meet the requirements of students completing their schooling and entering colleges or job market, or preparing for various competitions. It aims not only to provide rudimentary and elementary lessons on English grammar, but also to arm them with necessary tools for writing and speaking quality English. The book will also be a helpful tool in the hands of those who, wherever stationed, wish to polish their English.

Parts of speech and **tense**, I believe, are the most important tools for learning quality English, both written and spoken. Emphasis will, therefore, be on them. If we master **tense** and fully comprehend the **parts of speech**, we could be left free to delve deep on our own and enrich ourselves. Readers will, therefore, find that after dwelling at some length on **parts of speech**, a swift departure is made to **tense**. While discussing the fundamentals of grammar, special stress has been laid on these two aspects. Also, it is proposed to devote some pages on the specifics of spoken English with examples that will hardly require any explanation. There will be conversations of varying types and situations that will exemplify **how to speak, what to speak in a given situation.**

As English is an idiomatic language, an extensive chapter is devoted on idioms so that the reader is able to master them to help him speak attractive and authentic English. The language we speak and the manner in which we speak—"the words we use in our chosen language"—can make, or mar our prospects. And since we are dealing with English here, it is the English *we speak or write* that will have a direct and immediate bearing on our success or failure or at the rate of success or failure. Prepositions play a very important role in spoken English. Readers will find a comprehensive list of prepositions aimed at loosening some of the knots they find difficult to unknot. Parts of speech, tense, prepositions and idioms therefore constitute the kernel of grammatical explorations made in this book which, it is believed, will make the reading of grammar a little less cumbersome and more enjoyable exercise than it usually is.

A question is often asked these days by those keen to improve their English: which English are we supposed to learn? Earlier, in India and in most of the Commonwealth Countries, British English was the only English we needed to acquaint ourselves with; and we proudly declared it to be Oxford English. Things, with the arrival of computers, have radically altered. And with globalization having come to fore, American English (some would frown at the very expression) has made a strong impact on our knowledge or let-us-say our non-knowledge of English. A case of no love lost between British and American English is well made out by this observation of Oscar Wilde who described Britain and America as "two great countries *divided* by a common language" (italics mine). Americans regard British English as effete and English regard

American English as uncouth, foul and slangy. In spite of these hostilities (?), English language commands respect of the world. It is not within the scope of this book to discuss these differences. That will require a fresh foray.

But knowledge of fundamentals of grammar will not be complete unless we also acquire knowledge about some of the key elements of present day market oriented world. *Advertisement* plays a crucial role in today's economy. Therefore, some rudimentary knowledge is sought to be imparted. *Telegram*, though no longer in use in its conventional form and structure, deserves a look; so do *Circulars* and *Note Makings*. They are unlikely to ever become old fashioned or stale. Short chapters are devoted on them as well. *Précis writing* and *paragraph writing* are integral part of our linguistic exercises. These have been discussed at some length. *Auxiliaries* are an aid to writing good and faultless English. They constitute fundamentals of grammar and find a place of prominence, and so do *prefixes* and *suffixes* as they help us build words and substantially improve our vocabulary. Mastering them means you are on way to building vocabulary which needless to say adds to ability and stature. Letter writing, one may say, is the culminating point of our knowledge of a language. We learn fundamentals of grammar because we want to write good and quality English and what, if not letters, can demonstrate that knowledge better! So, you find them all here in some measure.

Computers have revolutionised our life. The age we are living in can easily be termed as *e*-age, with *e*-message, *e*-commerce and *e-governance* having become essential parts of our life. A brief chapter on that therefore becomes essential and is provided towards the end of the book to serve as an aid to understand computer English.

–N.C. Sinha

1A, Chitra Complex
Ambedkar Nagar
Patna-800 014
email: nimaisinha50@gmail.com

Contents

Sentence

Sentence: A sentence is a group of words or collection of words conveying a definite and grammatically correct meaning. In other words, a sentence must convey a *complete* sense in order to be called a sentence. The *sense* will be complete only when *something* is stated about *something* else.

The train left the station.

Types of sentence: Usually, there are four types of sentence. When something is stated merely to affirm or deny a thing or two, we have a statement. When there is an affirmation, the sentence is positive and when there is denial, it is negative.

Your destiny is in your own hand. (Affirmative)
I did not receive the kind of support that was due. (Negative)

When there is a request, a command, a wish or an entreaty, the sentence can be classified as **desire.**

Please do this for me. (Request)
Take the responsibility to accomplish the task. (Command)
May you achieve success in your life! (Wish)
Save our soul (SOS), we are drowning. (Entreaty)

When enquiries are made about something, this kind of sentence is called **questions** or **interrogatories.**

When did the train leave?

When some feelings are expressed, the sentence can be

classified as **exclamation.**

What a joy to have you in our midst!

Subject and **predicate** are the two parts of a sentence. The word denoting a person or a thing about which something is stated is called **subject** of the sentence.

The *train* left the station.

The word or words which state something about the thing or person denoted by the Subject as *left* in the sentence above is **predicate**.

Roughly speaking, the subject offers something for consideration, and the predicate offers some statement about it. In the sentences that follow the italicized parts are the **subject** and the remaining words constitute the **predicate:**

i) *The policeman* flogged the thief;
ii) *The thief with emaciated face* was constantly flogged by the policeman;
iii) *Rising* early is good for your health;
iv) Did *they* drive the car?

The **subject**, as can be seen, always contains a NOUN or something equivalent to that, while the **predicate** always a VERB. There will always be specific criteria for identifying the **subject** and the **predicate** in any language based usually on word order and inflexions.

It is equally imperative that in order to create a sentence that conveys a complete sense we must have both **subject** and **predicate**. They are mandatory for making of a sentence. Some examples can be given as under:-

Subject	**Predicate**
Rita	is a girl.
Cow	is an animal
Sweet	are the lessons of adversity
His parents	have arrived
Wages	have to be earned
Man days	are lost

Phrase: A phrase is a combination of words that makes *some* sense, but not *complete* sense. It is idiomatic in character and in form. *Above one's station* (higher than one's social class or standing), *a dog in the manger* (a selfish person), *acid test* (a test whose findings are beyond reproach or doubt/dispute), *through thick and thin* (through good times and bad times), *on the track* (seeking someone or something) are idioms. English, as we all know, is an idiomatic language.

Clause: A clause is a sentence, but always a part of a larger sentence. *This is the man who helped me out. This is the man* is a sentence because it has a subject in *this* and a predicate in *is.* Likewise, *who helped me out* is also a sentence because we have a subject in *who* and a predicate in *helped.* Since both of these sentences are parts of a larger sentence, each of them is called **clause**.

□

Parts of Speech

Each word is expected to serve a definite purpose. They are divided into different kinds or classes depending on the purpose they are assigned to serve. These different kinds of words are called **parts of speech.** They are eight in number and are briefly defined/explained (detailed explanations/definitions are given in the pages that follow) as under:

Noun is a naming word that is assigned the task of naming a person or a thing. Noun is name and name is noun. They can be used interchangeably.

Pronoun is the word that serves the purpose of a noun by substituting it. A pronoun is used in place of a noun or a noun-equivalent. The *train* left the station with all *her* seats taken. Here *train* the noun is substituted with *her* the pronoun to avoid repetitiveness. Pronoun is primarily a replacing or substituting word the function of which is to avoid repetitions.

Adjective is a restrictive word. It restricts the use or applicability of a noun, a pronoun or another adjective. When we say 'a horse' the reference is to any horse in the world. Its application is unrestricted or unlimited. But the moment we say a 'lame horse' the number gets restricted to just a few because there must be fewer 'lame horses' than normal 'horses'. **Adjectives** are therefore restrictive words, though the usual definition is— they qualify a noun or a pronoun or even an adjective. A *roaring* engine steamed out of the station. In the instant case, the adjective *roaring* adds quality to the noun *engine*. There may have been so many engines on the station, but perhaps only one *roaring* engine. In the instant case, therefore, our adjective performs the *adding* as well as *restrictive* role. It also plays an identifying role. In the instant example, the *engine* that is *roaring* is identified from amongst several engines. So, an **adjective** is also an **identifier**.

Verb is a predicating word. It says something about some person or thing. It is an action word. In the example *the train left the station,* the word *left* predicates or says something about the *train* the subject and therefore *left* is a verb, the predicate of the sentence, meaning thereby that the predicate of a sentence must be a verb or must at least have one in it.

Adverb does the same thing to verb that an adjective does to a noun or a pronoun. Verb as we know is a doing word or an action word. Now, how that action is performed, what is the status of performance is what an adverb tells us about. Just as an adjective qualifies a noun or a pronoun, an adverb qualifies a verb or anything except a noun or a pronoun.

The *very* roaring engine that left the station has *already* passed through *major* distance.

In the given example, *engine* is the noun that is qualified by the adjective *roaring.* This verbal adjective (it is made up from 'roar' which is a verb) is qualified by the adverb *very. Already* qualifies *passed* and *major* qualifies preposition *through.* According to some, *very* in the example will be regarded as an adjective qualifying the other adjective 'roaring', because they define an adverb as "a word used to qualify verbs, adjectives or other adverbs."

Preposition is a word that shows or establishes relationship between two objects or things. It shows how a thing is related to the other. For instance we have two objects *water* and *jug.* Unless we make use of a preposition, the objects on their own will make no sense, they do not say anything. But when we say, he carries water *in* his hand, we establish a relation between water and the hand and the meaning becomes intelligible to all. So, words such as *in, at, through, under and over* etc. are prepositions that establish relation between two or more things. Anything that follows the preposition is called its **object.** Obviously, what follows a preposition has to be noun, pronoun or noun-equivalent. Therefore, we may conclude that the use of preposition is to establish or show relation in which the person or thing denoted by its object stands to something else. **Preposition** is best explained by way of examples. They are: I live *in* Delhi, *near* Connaught Circus; who gave it *to* you? It was you that I gave it *to*. Prepositions are usually followed by a NOUN or a PRONOUN or its equivalent which they are said to govern, but in some cases (as in the third example) the preposition is separated from the word it governs. A preposition takes its position before a noun or a pronoun and establishes relation with some other words (usually an object) in the sentence.

Conjunction is a joining word. It joins words and phrases to one another, or one sentence to another.

A man is truly liberated *only when* he attains nirvana.
I detest him *simply because* he has bad manners.
We must first find out *precisely why* he chose to do this.
He reached the station *shortly before* the train arrived.
The bomb exploded *long after* the minister had left.
She has been in distress *ever since* her husband died.
Also
I have promises to keep *and* miles to go before I sleep.
She sometimes counsel takes *and* sometimes tea.
I could have done it, *but* she prevented me.
You have one choice *or* no choice at all.

Interjection is a mere sound and not word connected with other words. This sound stands on its own in a sentence and is there to express some feeling of the mind.

Oh! What a joy to have you in our midst!
Alas! She could not make it.
Fie upon you to have done this!

□

Noun

(Noun & its classification)

Old grammar

Proper	Common	Collective	Material	Abstract

New grammar

Proper	Countable	Uncountable

Noun is a word that names something, whether abstract (intangible) or concrete (tangible). It may be a common noun (the name of a generic class or type of person, place, or thing) or a proper noun (the formal name of a specific person, place or thing). A concrete noun may be a count noun (if what it names can be counted) or a mass noun (if what it names is uncountable or collective).

Common and **Collective** & **Material** and **Abstract** nouns of Old Grammar have become **Countable** and **Uncountable** respectively under New Grammar while **Proper Noun** has retained its pre-eminent position in both forms.

Proper Noun has a distinct personality of its own whether in the form of a person or in the form of a place. This distinct personality, place or person, retains its distinctiveness no matter where it occurs in a sentence. *Little did Akbar know that his distant generations will not count for much;* or, *whoever comes to Patna* *will regret having come.* Now in both of these sentences the proper noun occurs in the middle of the sentence, yet the nouns *Akbar* in the first and *Patna* in the second start with capital A and capital P. This rule has no exception. **Proper noun** is a personal name or the official name of a place or thing (Nayan Bagchi), (Gurgaon), (the Himalayas). It is always capitalized, regardless of how it is used. A common noun may become a proper noun (Nelson's flagship was the Victory), and sometimes a proper noun may be used figuratively and informally, as if it were a common noun (Natwarlal is a Napoleon of crime). Napoleon here connotes an ingenious mastermind who is ambitious beyond limits. Proper nouns may be compounded when used as a unit to name something (the Mourya Sheraton Hotel), (The Midday Journal). Overtime, some proper nouns (called **eponyms**) have developed common-noun counterparts, such as *sandwich* (from the Earl of Sandwich) and *China* (from the country of China). The word *boycott* is also a proper noun derivative, derived from the name of C.C. Boycott, an Irish land agent of early nineteenth century.

Common Noun is common to any and every thing or person of the same kind and it does not denote any particular person or a thing. History, man and nation are apt examples. When we speak of history, we do not speak of any particular history, history of Indian Freedom Struggle for instance. Likewise when we talk about man, we do not refer to any Akbar or Sebastian as definite individuals, and in the same way our reference to nation does not mean any particular nation. **Common noun** is the informal name of one item in a class or group (a chemical), (a river), (a pineapple). It is not capitalized unless it begins in a sentence or appears in a title.

Collective Noun is a collection or group of identical individuals regarded as one complete whole. Imagine a team of soccer players in a field. Now there are several *players* in the field but only one *team.* So, here player is common noun because he could be any player out of so many players present there, but 'team' is collective noun because it represents all players in one go. It is a collection of players where players are not taken separately. In New Grammar both Common Noun and Collective Noun are classified as **Countable Noun or Count Noun.** In the instant case, both players and teams can be counted. Therefore, they are also called **Countable Noun**. **Count noun** has singular and plural forms and expresses things that can be enumerated (dictionary-dictionaries), (hoof-hooves), (newspaper-newspapers). As the subject of a sentence, a singular count noun takes a singular verb (the jar is full); a plural count noun takes a plural verb (the jars are full).

Material Noun refers to the material or substance of which the thing is made. So while watch is a Common Noun, the steel of which it is made is Material Noun. Cow is a common noun while meat is a material noun. Fish is both common noun and material noun depending on usage and sense.

Fish abound in ponds. *Fish* is a palatable food.

While in the first sentence *fish* represents individual fish or fishes and is therefore common noun, in the second sentence *fish* represents matter or substance its body is made up or and is therefore material noun.

Abstract Noun denotes some quality, status or action. Anything intangible can be called Abstract Noun. While bravery, fortitude, honesty, humility etc. speak of quality; poverty, pleasure, sorrow, youth speak of status and fancy, revenge, gratitude speak of action. Both material and abstract nouns are **Uncountable** under New Grammar. We can count pieces of steel, but not steel. We may count the acts of bravery, but not bravery itself. They are, therefore, **Uncountable.** Material and abstract nouns can be clubbed together as mass noun.

Mass noun, often called non-count noun or a collective noun is one that denotes something uncountable, either because it is abstract: cowardice, evidence; or, because it refers to an indeterminate aggregation of people or things: the faculty, the collegiums. As the subject of a sentence, a mass noun usually takes a singular verb: the government is under siege. But in a collective sense, it may take either a singular or a plural verb form: the ruling party is unlikely to share power; the majority of the voters are satisfied. A singular verb emphasizes the group; a plural verb emphasizes the individual members. If a collective noun appears throughout a piece of writing, use one verb form consistently.

Countable and uncountable nouns

Maximum number of nouns belongs to the category of **COUNTABLE** nouns and **UNCOUNTABLE** nouns or **MASS** nouns. Most of the countable nouns are words for distinct things that can be counted, like *bricks*, *books* and *bikes*. Uncountable nouns are words that tell of a quantity or mass, like *gas* and *sunshine*. But then, there are some nouns that we perceive as countable, but are not so. For instance, *information, furniture, aircraft* and *equipment* are uncountable nouns in English and they do not takes to become plural.

Nouns have four properties: case, gender, number and person.

Case: In English, only nouns and pronouns have case. Case denotes the relationship between a noun or pronoun and other words in a sentence. Three cases are: nominative, objective and possessive. Except in the possessive, nouns do not change form to indicate case. Examples: the *doctor* is in (nominative case); see the *doctor* (objective case), but the *doctor's* chamber (possessive case).

Gender: Classifies nouns into masculine, feminine, and neuter. In English, the masculine and feminine genders occur almost exclusively with (1) nouns that refer to male or female humans or animals (boy), (girl), (horse), (mare); (2) compound nouns that contain specifically masculine or feminine nouns or pronouns (fisherman), (watchman), (housewife); (3) nouns that have a feminine suffix such as *ess* or *ix* (many of which are not in use now having become archaic) such as *actress, executrix*; and (4) nouns used in personification. Almost all other words are neuter (monarch) (sheep), (government). If gender is to be indicated, descriptive adjectives such as male and female may be needed if there is no gender specific term: for example, a female fox is a *vixen*, but there is no equivalent term for a female goldfish.

Number: Shows whether one object or more than one object is referred to, as with *bicycle* (singular) and *bicycles* (plural). Strictly speaking, the only nouns that can be used as plurals are common and collective nouns, and one of the simplest ways of forming plurals is by addition of *s* to a noun; as–

Singular	**plural**	**singular**	**plural**
Stone	stones	shoe	shoes
Cradle	cradles	mat	mats

Where nouns end with *s, sh, ch, x, es* is added to make them plural; as–

Singular	**plural**	**singular**	**plural**
Class	classes	Trash	trashes
Wrench	wrenches	wax	waxes

Nouns ending with *y* when it is preceded by consonant, *y* is replaced with ies to form plural; as–

Singular	**plural**	**singular**	**plural**
Sky	skies	fly	flies
Duty	duties	beauty	beauties
Lady	ladies	sentry	sentries

But when *y* is preceded by vowel, it takes simple *s* as in the case of *day* becoming *days, boy* becoming *boys, toy* becoming toys and *play* becoming *plays.* Likewise, when noun ends with *o* and it is preceded with consonant, *es* is generally added to make plurals; as–

Singular	**plural**	**singular**	**plural**
Hero	heroes	zero	zeroes
Mango	mangocs	buffalo	buffaloes
Cargo	cargoes	Negro	Negroes
Potato	potatoes	tomato	tomatoes
Tornado	tornadoes	echo	echoes
Volcano	volcanoes		

Some of the exceptions in this category are:

Singular	**plural**	**singular**	**plural**
Ego	egos	halo	halos
Solo	solos	credo	credos
Memento	mementos	piano	pianos
Proviso	provisos		

Some nouns ending with *oo, io, eo* or *yo* take *s* to become plural; as–

Singular	plural	singular	plural
Bamboo	bamboos	cuckoo	cuckoos
Embryó	embryos	imbroglio	imbroglios
Curio	curios	folio	folios
Cameo	cameos	portfolio	portfolios

There are some exceptions in this category too. Some nouns ending with *o* take both *s* and *es* as:

Singular	plural
Mosquito	mosquitos/mosquitoes
Portico	porticos/porticoes

There are some nouns ending with *f* and *fe* change to *ves* for acquiring plural hue; as–

Singular	plural	singular	plural
Calf	calves	half	halves
Knife	knives	life	lives
Leaf	leaves	thief	thieves
Elf	elves	shelf	shelves
Yourself	yourselves	wife	wives
Wolf	wolves	golf	gloves

But there are exceptions to this rule as well. Those ending with *f*:

Chief	chiefs	roof	roofs
Dwarf	dwarfs	scarf	scarfs/scarves
Kerchief	kerchiefs	cliff	cliffs
Grief	griefs/grieves	proof	proofs
Hoof	hoofs/hooves	turf	turfs

Those ending with *fe* and the only known exceptions are:

Safe	safes	fife	fifes
Strife	strifes (strives is its verb form)		

There are some nouns that change inwardly such as *man* becoming *men*, *woman* becoming *women*, *foot* becoming *feet*, *tooth* becoming *teeth*, *goose* becoming *geese*, *mouse* becoming *mice*, *louse* becoming *lice*, etc. And then there are some nouns that take *en* or *ne* to make plural, as *brother* becoming *brethren*, *child* becoming *children, cow* becoming *kine* or *cows, ox* becoming *oxen.*

Numbers (cardinals and ordinals) are shown in figures and words as under:

Cardinal		**Ordinal**	
Figure	Word	Figure	Word
1	one	1st	first
2	two	2nd	second
3	three	3rd	third
4	four	4th	fourth
5	five	5th	fifth
6	six	6th	sixth
7	seven	7th	seventh
8	eight	8th	eighth
9	nine	9th	nineth
11	eleven	11th	eleventh
21	twenty-one	21st	twenty-first
30	thirty	30th	thirtieth
51	fifty-one	51st	fifty-first
101	one hundred one	101st	one hundred first

Additional information on the fundamental rules for forming of plurals.

Majority of plurals, as shown above, are formed with the addition of *s* or *es.* If a noun ends with a letter whose sound readily combines with the sound of *s*, then use *s* to form plural: *pen-pens, bat-bats, girl-girls.* If the noun ends with a letter that is not euphonious with *s* alone (for example, it ends with a sibilant such as s, *sh, x, z,* or a soft *ch*), then use *es* to make it plural: *fox-foxes, flash-flashes, church-churches.*

Some of the nouns ending, as seen above, in *f* take an *s* to make plural: *roof-roofs, dwarf-dwarfs, chief-chiefs.* Others change *f* to *v* and take *es* to make plurals: *wife-wives, knife-knives, hoof-hooves* and *wolf-wolves.*

Nouns ending in *o*, as demonstrated above, take an *s* such as *credo-credos, memento-mementos* and *tuxedo-tuxedos.* But others take an *es* such as *mango-mangoes, cargo-cargoes, flamingo-*

flamingoes and *volcano-volcanoes.* There is no firm rule for determining whether the plural is formed with *s* or *es*, but two guidelines may prove useful: 1) Nouns used as often in the plural as in the singular usually form plural with *es: veto-vetoes, hero-heroes.* 2) Nouns usually form plural with *s* if they appear to have been borrowed from some other language *(imbroglio-imbroglios)*; if they are proper names such as *Romeo-Romeos* and *Fazio-Fazios;* if they are seldom used as plurals such as *bravado-bravados;* if they end in *o* preceded by a vowel such as *portfolio-portfolios;* or if they are shortened words such as *photo-photos.*

Nouns ending in *y* follow one of the two rules: 1) If the noun is common and *y* is preceded by *qu* or by a consonant, change the *y* to *i* and add *es* to form the plural. Some such examples in addition to already shown above are: *soliloquy-soliloquies, ferry-ferries, berry-berries, folly-follies* and *trolly-trollies.* 2) If the noun is proper or if *y* is preceded by a vowel, add *s* to form the plural such as *Teddy-Teddys, Reddy-Reddys, boy-boys, toy-toys, ploy-ploys* or *buoy-buoys.*

Compound nouns that consist of separate words (with or without hyphens) form the plural by adding the appropriate ending to the noun or, if there is more than one, to the main noun such as *brother-in-law–brothers-in-law*, *court-martial–courts-martial* or *motion-picture–motion-pictures.* In the last example, *picture* is made into plural because this is the main noun and not the first word *motion* which is not the main noun.

Some nouns have irregular plurals such as *child-children, oasis-oases, basis-bases* or *thesis-theses.* With some of these irregular words, the plural form depends on the meaning. For instance, *louse* becomes *lice* when people are affected with it, but contemptible people are *louses* (by metaphorical extension). Some nouns are ordinarily the same in both the singular and the plural, especially those denoting *fish, game* and *livestock,* etc.

Some nouns are plural in form but singular in use and meaning such as the good *news* is, *politics* is a complex subject, *mathematics* is easy to understand or *physics* is not so easy.

Person shows whether an object is speaking (first person) as in—*we* will decide, *we* is the first person in plural number. It shows whether an object is spoken to (second person) as in—boys, stand up, *boys* is the second person), or whether an object is spoken about (third person) as in—a monkey took the loaf, *monkey* and *loaf* are in the third person. The chart given below will illustrate the working of person and number:

	Singular	Plural
1st person	I play.	We play.
2nd person	You play.	You play.
3rd person	He/she plays.	They play.

□

Pronoun

Chulain saw a *hound* at the gate, this *hound, Chulain* knew, would not let *Chulain* pass until *Chulain* overpowered the *hound* with all the power and strength *Chulain* could command.

This is an attempt to make a sentence without using any pronoun. The result is what you see. The sentence not only looks clumsy and irksome, but also overly repetitive. Here comes the utility of pronoun. The same sentence can be re-written with the help of pronouns in this way:

Chulain saw a hound at the gate which *he* knew would not let him pass until *he* overpowered it with all the power and strength *he* could command.

You can breathe easy as you read this. This then is the function of a pronoun. It saves you the trouble of having to repeat nouns in a sentence every now and then. From the above, it becomes plain that: 1) since a pronoun is used in place of a noun, it must itself be a noun or a noun-equivalent, 2) since the pronoun is intended to be a substitute of a preceding noun, no pronoun can be mentioned until a noun has actually been mentioned earlier, 3) since a pronoun is used in place of a noun, it must be of the same number, gender and person as the noun preceding it. While pronouns have functions similar to those of nouns, they also differ from them in some ways. For instance, they cannot be preceded by *the* or by adjectives. There are various sub-groups as under:

i) Personal Pronoun as *I, you, he, she;*

ii) Demonstrative Pronoun as *this, that, one, such* (in sentences like '*This* is what I meant', 'I don't like *that*');

iii) Relative Pronoun as *who, which, that, as* (in sentences like 'I know the man who killed her,' 'She brought a camera which she carried away with her');

iv) Interrogative Pronoun as *Whom? Which? What?* (in sentences like 'Who knows?' 'Which one will you take?' 'What will you do?');

v) Indefinite Pronoun as *none, any, each* and

vi) Reflexive and Intensive Pronoun as *myself, himself, ourselves* etc.

□

Adjective

(Adjective & its kinds)

Further to what has already been stated, an adjective can simply be defined as a *word that is used to qualify a noun or a pronoun.* But it can be variously described as a qualifying or a restricting word. When a word describes a noun or a pronoun either by pointing out some of its qualities (the *thick* cloud, the *beaten* rice, a *long* speech) or restricting or limiting its reference (the *living* legend, Ten *Commandments*, the *first* folio, the *lame* horse), we have an adjective. Although, grammarians usually give us eight kinds of adjectives, in fact, adjectives are mainly of two kinds:

1) descriptive adjectives
2) limiting or restrictive adjectives also called determiners.

Adjectives that single out the quality of a person or a thing or an idea in order to describe are descriptive and they tell us about what kind of a person, a thing or an idea is referred to:

- an *angry* young man (describing the quality of a young man);
- a *broken* window (stating the status of a window which is a broken one);
- an *absurd* idea (describes an idea that is absurd).

Limiting or restrictive adjectives (or determiners as they also called) limit or restrict the use of noun or pronoun. They usually refer to *which* or *how many* persons, things or ideas are referred to or are there:

- *This* building (which building is referred to? *This* building);
- Only *one* man (how many men were alluded to? *One*);

- The *second* apartment (which apartment? The *second* apartment).

Some of these descriptive adjectives because of their special endings are easy to identify. Here are some samples:

-ful : grateful, forgetful, deceitful, and beautiful
-less : graceless, shameless, cloudless, and meaningless
-able : portable, charitable, hospitable, and acceptable
-ible : incorrigible, edible, terrible, and irresistible
-en : silken, woollen, swollen, and golden
-al : natural, musical, medical, and radical
-ous : victorious, glorious, and mischievous
-ive : descriptive, prescriptive, and imaginative
-ic : poetic, euphoric, historic, and heroic
-ish : English, childish, and selfish
-some : handsome, lonesome, quarrelsome, and troublesome
-ary/ery : imaginary, customary, and voluntary, stationery, stationary
-ly : scholarly, lonely, manly, and friendly
-y : milky, dirty, silky, and shaky

But then, there are other descriptive adjectives that have no special endings for easy identification. Some of them are: *old, young, large, long, short, hard, white, black, soft, quick, rich, bad, hot,* and *cold.*

Limiting or restrictive adjectives or determiners include the following:

a) Articles (a, an, the)

There is *a* patient in *the* operation theatre. *The* patient is seriously ill.

(How many patients are there? A patient = one patient. Where is he? In the operation theatre. Which one (who=wh+o) is seriously ill? The patient, i.e. the only one person who is a patient).

Articles are three in number: *a, an, the.* While *the* is a definite article because it particularises a noun, *a* and *an* are indefinite articles because they generalise a noun, i.e. they apply to any of the same class or genre. Articles, however, are not a distinct part of speech. They are rather adjectives. *A* and *an* are the same thing except that while *a* precedes consonant, *an* precedes vowel and both of them are abbreviated forms of *one* and therefore called *indefinite articles.* In the same way *the* is the abbreviated form of *this, that, these* and *those* and since all of them are demonstrative in character, they are *definite articles.* A thing is said to be of demonstrative character when it points to something definite and that is the characteristic of a demonstrative adjective.

b) Demonstrative adjectives: this, that, these and those are called demonstrative adjectives because they point to the things, persons or ideas that are referred to. For instance: *This* building is taller than *that* building; *these* men are smarter than *those* men.

c) Possessive adjectives are *my, your, his, her, our, their, its, mine.* They are called possessive because they show ownership or possession.
His house... (Which house is being referred to? The house he possesses).
Your saucer... (Which saucer is being referred to? The saucer you possess).

d) Interrogative adjectives are *what, which,* and *whose* and these are used with nouns to ask questions:
What size is your vest?
Which way will you go?
Whose house is this?

e) Quantifiers are those that take into their ambit the traditional quantitative and numeral adjectives such as *four, forty, some, much, all, several.* They either indicate definite numerical quantities (*four* musketeers, *forty* thieves, *fifty-one* pieces) and indefinite quantities (a *few* morsels, *most* services, *some* exercises) or make distributive references (*either* way, *each* day, *neither* party, *every* piece of information).

f) Relative adjectives and relative pronouns are identical in as much as they link dependent clauses or subordinate clauses to the main or principal clauses. But while relative pronouns link the clauses by replacing the nouns, relative adjectives achieve the same objective by modifying the nouns.
Some of the colloquial adjective phrases used extensively in conversations are as under:

A *jack-of-all-trades* (all-knowing or all-doing, no specialization) man; a *jack-in-the-box* (volatile) man; a *go-ahead* (pushing or aggressive) person; a *good-for-nothing* (useless, incompetent) man; a *stick-in-the-mud* (not enterprising or not pushing) man; a *happy-go-lucky* (haphazard) plan; a *stay-at-home* (domestic, indoor) person; a *dog-in-the-manger* (selfish) doctrine; an *upside-down* (inverted) idea; an *out-of-the-way* (secluded) place; an *out-of-doors* (open air) assignment.

□

Verb

Verb is an action word and appears as the predicate in a sentence. A verb is **finite** when any part of it can be used as the *predicate of a sentence.* It is 'finite' because it is 'limited' to the same person (First, Second or Third person) and the same number (Singular or Plural) as its subject. But there are some parts of a verb which are not limited to any particular number or person in view of their inability of being used with a subject or as the predicate of a sentence and are, therefore, **Infinite**. Their uses are **Infinitive** as "she desires *to secede*"; a **Partici ple**, as "*a seceded country*"; a **Gerund**, as "she thinks of *seceding*". A Partici ple can also be seen as the combination of a verb and an adjective.

A *seceded* country is not easy to deal with.

The word *seceded* is a verb but it qualifies the noun country and is therefore an adjective. So in the given example the word *seceded* is both a verb and an adjective. A **Partici ple** is accordingly called a *verbal adjective.* A **Gerund** on the other hand is the combination of a verb and noun.

Tamil Elam thinks of *seceding* from Sri Lanka.

In the given example, the word *seceding* is a verb because it is part of the verb *secede.* It is also a noun because it is the object to the preposition *of.* Accordingly, gerund has also been called a *verbal noun.*

Transitive, Intransitive and **Auxiliary** are three types of verb. A verb is said to be **Transitive** when the action or a notion of it denoted by the verb does not end at itself, rather progresses towards some person or thing. Words denoting such person or thing are called **Object** to the verb.

The bullet hit *the terrorist.*

If the sentence had ended with the verb *hit*, we would have been groping for meaning. But once it hit the terrorist, the action is said to have passed on to its (bullet's) object, i.e. the terrorist. The sense is complete and the verb is **Transitive**. But there are actions that do not search for an object to make their sense clear. A verb is **Intransitive** when the action or the notion of it stops at itself and does not progress towards any object.

We *live* Birds *fly* Children *play* Wind *blows*

While **intransitive** verbs do not require an **object**, at times they require a **complement**, as **transitive** verbs also occasionally do. Such verbs can be categorised as *Intransitive Verbs of Incomplete Predication.*

Here comes a *Good Samaritan.* Smoking is *injurious to health.*

While transitive verb has two voices: **active** and **passive**, intransitive verb is not used in passive voice except when it takes a cognate [(of a word) having the same linguistic family or derivation] object in the active. It is **active voice** when a person or a thing denoted by the subject is said to be doing something to some other thing or object. **Voice** will be discussed at length in the chapter relating to Tense.

Hari *carries* a ball.

In the instant case, the subject Hari does something to a ball the object. He carries it. It is **active voice** here; but when the person or a thing is said to be at the receiving or at the suffering end, it is **passive voice**.

A goat is *hunted* by the tiger.

Here the goat the subject is at the receiving end or at the suffering end as it suffers from the tiger. The first example can also be turned into a passive voice:

A ball is carried by Hari.

As stated above, an **intransitive verb** is not used in passive voice except when it takes a cognate object in the active.

I have fought the good fight. (Active)

The good fight has been fought by me. (Passive)

As can be seen from the above, the subject in the Active Voice has become object in the Passive Voice and object in the Active Voice has become subject in the Passive Voice.

Auxiliary verb is a helping verb and it does so by forgoing its own significance in a sentence. It assists the main verb as can be seen in the given sentence:

He *has* performed a great feat.

In the given example *has* is an Auxiliary verb that has lost its own meaning of 'possession' in order to assist the main verb 'performed' to complete the present perfect tense. *Shall, will, should, would, have,* etc. are some of the assisting verbs known as **Auxiliary Verb**. A separate chapter is devoted to auxiliaries.

□

Adverb

(Adverb and its types)

A**dverb** is usually known to have been defined as a word that qualifies a verb, an adjective or other adverb. More precisely, it was identified as a word that stated the *position* or *status* of an action. But Nesfield defined it as a word that qualified any part of speech except noun or pronoun. Since Interjection stood on its own, an adverb could also qualify a preposition and a conjunction. Here is an example of how it qualifies a preposition followed by another example of how it qualifies a conjunction:

The wind blew *swiftly over* my head. (*swiftly*-adverb, *over*-preposition)

and

He has been ruined *ever since* he deserted us. (Conjunction)

Adverbs can be sub-divided into the following categories:

1. Simple 2. Interrogative 3. Relative

Simple Adverbs: Depending on their meaning, these can be exemplified as under:

It blossomed *now* (Time). Main adverbs belonging to this class are:

Today, tomorrow, yesterday, before, presently, immediately, early, late and soon.

Please go *there* (Place). Some of the chief adverbs in this category are:

Here, in, out, within, without, far, near, above, below, inside, outside etc.

He failed *twice* (Number). Chief adverbs under this category are:

Once, twice, regularly, again, never, sometimes, often, always, seldom, etc.

She did it *slowly* but *efficiently* (Manner). Some of the key adverbs in this category are:

Properly, certainly, probably, thus, so, well, ill, amiss, badly, etc.

They have *nearly* but not *exactly* accomplished the task. (Extent/ Degree/Quantum).

Some of the notable adverbs under this category are:

Very, much, too, quite, almost, little, a little, few, a few, half, partly, wholly, etc.

He could not do it *ultimately* (Affirmation/Denial).

To this category belong the following adverbs:

Yes, no, not, nay, yeah, not at all, by all means, etc.

Interrogative Adverbs:

This nomenclature is used for those adverbs that are used for asking questions:

When, why, what, how long, wherefore, whence, whether, whither, etc.

Relative Adverbs:

These are identical to Interrogative adverbs in form; but instead of asking questions, these adverbs serve the purpose of joining sentences together as conjunctions do. Relative Adverbs are also known as double parts of speech–a combination of adverb and conjunction. There are two reasons why a relative adverb is so-called. One, because it relates to some antecedent (preceding thing or occurrence), expressed or understood, like relative pronouns. Two, because it is formed out of relative pronoun. Let us understand by way of some examples:

a) Where the antecedent is understood:

This is *where* (the house or the place in which) Premchand lived.

Let us see *when* (the time by which) the train arrives.

b) Where the antecedent is expressed:

This is the place or house *where* Premchand lived.

Let us see the time *when* the train arrives.

□

Preposition

A **Preposition** is a word that is placed before a noun or noun-equivalent to establish in what relation with the person or thing denoted by it stands to something else. The noun or noun-equivalent is known as object.

She placed the book *on* the table.

In the above example if we omit the word 'on', the sentence will make no sense. The exact position of the book in relation to the table is known because of the preposition 'on'. The book could well have been 'under' the table, or 'above' the table. Mere use of a preposition has removed all possible confusion about the location of the book by firmly establishing the relation between the book and the table. This is what is the function of preposition.

The six different forms of preposition are discussed below:

a) **Simple Prepositions** are: at, *by, with, on, in, for, to, off, or, of, through, from, up, over, till, after* and *under* etc.

b) **Double Prepositions** are used when a single preposition does not serve the desired purpose or when they fail to fully express the sense intended: The frog fell *into* the well. He is king *unto* himself. I was attacked *from behind.* The task fell *onto* him. The rug was pulled *from under* his feet. She was selected *from among* the best.

c) **Compound Prepositions** are made up by compounding noun, adjective or adverb with the preposition: *amongst, across, along, amidst, behind, between, betwixt, above, about, before, within, without,* *below, beneath, beside, beyond*, *but*, etc.

d) Participial Prepositions: These prepositions were originally present or past partici ples used absolutely, occasionally with noun expressed and occasionally with some nouns understood.

Some examples when noun is expressed:

The hour *past* midnight (the hour, midnight *having passed).*

All *save* one or all *except* one (all, one *being saved* or *preserved* and all, one *being excepted*).

Notwithstanding his loss (his loss not-*withstanding* or not preventing his loss).

Examples when noun is understood:

Owing to incessant rains and release of water by Nepal, Bihar was flooded.

Considering the constraints they had to face, it must be conceded that they have done a great job.

Weighing the pros and cons of the matter, it was the right decision to make.

e) Phrase Prepositions are also called prepositional phrases.

When two or more words habitually or in a matter of course are put together ending with a simple preposition, they are called prepositional phrases or phrase prepositions. Examples are innumerable: *In lieu of, instead of, by means of, by dint of, because of, in front of, in spite of, on account of, in place of, for the sake of, in the event of, with reference to, on behalf of,* etc.

f) Disguised Prepositions: When we say four o'clock, we actually say four of clock. Here 'of' is disguised in 'o'. Likewise, there are occasions when 'by' is disguised in 'be' and 'on' is disguised in 'a' by way of a prefix to a certain nouns or adjectives. When we say 'meat sells at one hundred twenty rupees *a kilo'*, *a* almost takes the shape of the indefinite article which it is not, but is disguised as one. By this false analogy, *the* is sometimes used mistakenly. In addition to *a* and *the*, *than* and *but* are also disguised prepositions.

A section will be devoted on words followed by prepositions to understand the correct usages of prepositions.

□

Conjunction

As has already been explained in the previous section, **Conjunction** is a word for joining. It is used for no other purpose. It is not connected with an object as in the case of preposition. It does not qualify a word as an adverb does. It simply joins a word or a sentence. Consequently, the same word can be an adverb in one place, a preposition in another and a conjunction in yet another. For instance:

I have met her *before.* (Adverb)

She stood *before* the gate. (Preposition)

The train left *before* she reached the station. (Conjunction)

Conjunctions can be divided into **Coordinating** and **Subordinating** conjunctions. Those that join sentences of equal rank or importance are called **Coordinating** conjunctions, and those that join a subordinate or dependent sentence to a sentence of higher rank or importance, rather to a principal sentence, are called **Subordinating** conjunctions. Now, sentences of equal rank or importance can be joined 1) by simply *adding* to another (**Cumulative**); 2) by *offering* an alternative or choice between one statement and another (**Alternative**); 3) by *contrasting* one statement or fact with or setting against another (**Adversative**) and 4) by *drawing inference* from one statement/fact or *proving* one statement/fact from another (**Illative**).

Coordinating Conjunctions

Under the category of **Cumulative** conjunction, we have the following examples:

And- The committee received the report, *and* the *secretariat* the recommendation.

Both...and- He was *both* rewarded *and* eulogised publicly.

Also- Harry is reprimanded, and Sania *also.*

Too- He is a smoker and a boozer *too.*

As well as- You *as well as* your brother are to blame for this.

Now- They decided to wait for the train; *now*, the train was not expected today.

Not only...but also- He is *not only* dishonest, *but also* of foul intent.

No less than- He was praised by *no less* a person *than* the prime minister himself.

Well The work was done efficiently by him; *well,* it was not expected of him.

Under the category of **Alternative** conjunction, we have the following examples:

Either...or- *Either* you have erred, *or* your brother has.

Neither...nor- *Neither* you have visited him, *nor* have you tried to contact him.

Else- Go away, *else* you will be picked up by the police.

Or- Perform *or* perish.

Otherwise- Perform this task; *otherwise*, we have to look for other options.

Under the category of **Adversative** conjunction, we have the following examples:

But- He is down, *but* not out.

Yet- She has won the battle, *yet* she is not satisfied.

Still- He is rich; *still*, he yearns for more.

Nonetheless- We have done it; *nonetheless,* we are not lowering our guard.

Nevertheless- They all voted against him; *nevertheless,* he won.

However- We all tried to reason with him; he, *however*, stuck to his theory.

While- Make hay *while* the sun shines.

Whereas- They all stayed indoors, *whereas* he chose to stay out.

Only- Do it as you wish, *only* do not overdo it.

Under the category of **Illative** conjunction, we have the following examples:

For- It takes ages to build an empire; *for*, Rome was not built in a day.

Therefore- He was found not guilty of the charge; *therefore*, he was let off.

Then- It is important to finish the work expeditiously; let us start *then*.

Subordinating Conjunctions

A sentence is said to be subordinate to another when it depends upon the other. In other words, when it enters into its construction with the force of a noun, adjective or adverb, it is said to be subordinate to the other. The **Dependent** sentence is that to which a subordinate conjunction is prefixed and the **Principal** sentence is that to which on which the subordinate or the inferior sentence depends. While this will also be elaborately explained under **Structures** and **Conditional statements**, the following example will illustrate the point:

Principal	**Conjunction**	**Dependent**
He will do the job	if	you ask him to.

A sentence can be made to depend on another in the following nine ways:

1) **Apposition** (used in an introductory sense):

Principal	**Dependent**
The school notified	*that* the admission to all (a statement of fact) classes was on.
They informed us	*that* they were to accomplish (to the effect) the task.

What comes under **Dependent** is in apposition with the noun shown in brackets which could either be expressed or left unexpressed.

2) Cause or Reason:

Principal	**Dependent**
The train will arrive now	*because* the track has been repaired.
She will do it	*since* you have asked her to.
Let us go then, you and I	*when* the evening is spread out against the sky.

3) Effect:

Principal	**Dependent**
He put in so much labour	*that* he fell sick.
She spoke so loudly	*that* she ruptured her vocal cord.

4) Purpose:

Principal	**Dependent**
She walked with a stick	*lest* she should fall.
We work	*that* we may earn our livelihood.
Dad took appetizer	*that* he might get hungry and eat.
We take regular exercises	*that* we might keep good health.

5) Condition:

Principal	**Dependent**
You have to do this work	*whether* or not you wish to.
I shall not do it	*until* I am paid for it.
She will come	*if* she is allowed to.
I agree to execute these	*provided* you propose it officially.
He gave a violent start	*as if* he was fired at.

6) Concession or Contrast:

Principal	**Dependent**
He will not take this money	*although* or *though* he is in dire need of it.

She will never agree *however* hard you pursue.
They will not win the war *however* much they try.
Pritam will not be content *however* rich he may have become.

I shall not take rest *till* I complete the assigned work.
She did not look fresh *notwithstanding* the fact that she had a shower.

It is important to mention here that conjunction *however* has twin functions: it coordinates and also subordinates. While coordinating, it stands alone in the middle of a sentence, generally; but while subordinating, it is usually placed at the beginning of a sentence and is invariably attached to some adverb as *hard, much* or to an adjective like *rich,* etc.

7) **Comparison:** This could be of two degrees: **Equal degrees** and **Unequal degrees.**

Equal degrees

The same quality compared:

She is *as slow as* I (am).
He loves you *as much as* I (love you).
My mother cares for you *no less than* me (she cares for me).

Different qualities compared:

The Antarctica is *as cold as* the Sun is *hot.*
The Himalayas is *as high as* the ocean is *deep.*
He is *as good as* he is *intelligent* (he is good and intelligent in equal measure)

Unequal Degrees

The same quality compared:

You are *more* (or *less*) active than I (am).
She loves you *more* (or *less*) than I (love you).
She loves you *more* (or *less*) than me (she loves me).

Different qualities compared:

The sun is hotter than the Antarctica is cold.
The Himalayas is higher than the ocean is deep.
He is more intelligent than (he is) good.

He is less intelligent than (he is) good.

8) Manner or Extent

Principal	**Dependent**
We will reap	*as* we sow (to what extent or in what manner).
This is not the case	*as far as* it is publicly known.
He chose them	*according as* they were eligible.
Principal	**Dependent**
As you sow,	*so* will you reap.

□

Interjections

About Interjections it can be safely said that it is merely an exclamatory sound, bereft of any meaning having a bearing on the sentence. It is just thrown into a sentence to convey some strong feeling or emotion. Strictly speaking, it is not a part of speech since it does not have any grammatical connection with any other word or words in a given sentence. It stands on its own. To express joy, we have *hurray*, *hurrah* or *huzza*. For expressing grief we have *oh, ah, alas, alack,* etc., *ha, ho* for amusement. *Bravo* for expressing approval, *heigh-ho* for registering weariness, *fie, fie* for showing disgust and reproof, *pooh-pooh* for showing contempt and *lo, hi, halo* for drawing attention.

□

Tense

Tense, as I have stated earlier, along with parts of speech, is the most important tool for learning quality English. Master these, you have mastered English. Tense means time and it shows 1) *time* of an action and 2) *status* of an action or *degree of its completeness.* Since action necessarily relates to verb, Tense therefore deals with verb. The verb tells us:

a) That an action is performed at the present time; as, 'she watches a game.'
b) That an action was performed in the past time; as, 'she watched a game.'
c) That an action will be performed in the future time; as, 'she will watch a game.'
d) That an action, at some time past, was viewed as future (Future in the Past); as, 'she would have watched a game.'

An action or a verb has four main times or tenses: the present, the past, the future and future in the past. Each of these get further divided into i) indefinite or simple, ii) continuous or progressive, iii) perfect and iv) perfect continuous or progressive.

Indefinite is the simplest form of time expressed in present, past, future and future in the past as "I play", "I played", "I shall play" and "I should play". It is, therefore, also called **Simple** past, present, future and simple future in the past. When a thing is done as a matter of course or habit or if a thing is universally acknowledged as a certainty like 'the sun rises in the east', this is indefinite or simple. In the example "I play" makes no reference to time, but to an action that is performed routinely or habitually.

Hence it is indefinite or simple: simple present (I play), simple past (I played) and simple future (I shall play).

Continuous or progressive denotes continuity of an event and is expressed in present, past, future and future in the past as "I am playing", "I was playing", "I shall be playing" and "I should be playing". In American grammar, continuous becomes progressive. So present continuous becomes present progressive, present perfect continuous becomes present perfect progressive. The same thing is for past and future.

Perfect denotes completion of an event and is expressed in present, past, future and future in the past as "I have played", "I had played", "I shall have played" and "I should have played".

Perfect continuous or progressive combines the attributes of both continuous and perfect of an event in part and is expressed in present, past, future and future in the past as "I have been playing", "I had been playing" and "I shall have been playing" and "I should have been playing". An action has commenced but not concluded is said to be in perfect continuous or progressive.

□

Uses of Tense

The present

The present continuous or progressive is used:

To speak of an action that is occurring now, or states about a temporary situation:

- ♦ They are **laying** chess board.
- ♦ What **is** he **doing**?
- ♦ He is not **responding** to my call.
- ♦ I am **repairing** this music system.
- ♦ She is **having** her lunch.

To speak of an action that is not yet finished, even if it is not actually being performed at the moment:

- ♦ He is **training** for handicraft.
- ♦ She is **running** for this post.
- ♦ I am **writing** a book on grammar.
- ♦ She is **doing** a cinema.

To speak of a thing or two that keeps happening and is irritating to you:

- ♦ She is **having** her lunch.
- ♦ She is always **pestering** me with requests for help.
- ♦ He is always **asking** those funny little questions.
- ♦ They are always **demanding** some kind of help from me.
- ♦ You are always **distracting** me with your antics.

It is important to note that some verbs like *need, want, know, agree, seem, smell, hear, appear, understand,* etc. are not used in continuous or progressive tenses. They do not refer to any action; rather they refer to a state.

- She is **having** her lunch.
- I **want** some rest.
- She **needs** some guidance.
- Does he **know** Sania Mirza?
- He **hates** the game of cricket.
- They **appear** lost.

Likewise, there are some verbs that, when used in present continuous or progressive tense, refer to an action; but they refer to a state when used in present simple tense:

- They **appear** lost.
- What are you **talking** about?
- Do you wish to **talk** to me?
- This fruit **tastes** sour.
- Should you like to **taste** it?

The present simple is used:

To speak of a situation of permanent nature or about something that is usually always true:

- Should you like to **taste** it?
- He **works** in the army.
- I **live** at Patna.
- Tigers **have** deadly claws.
- Antarctica **is** a cold continent.

To speak about things that happen on regular basis and there is little scope for change:

- Should you like to **taste** it?
- He **goes** to his chamber at 7 in the evening.
- I **go** to my office at 9 in the morning.
- She **takes** 9.15 train everyday without fail.
- We **go** for morning walk at 5 o'clock.

The past

The past simple is used:

To speak of an action that took place sometime in the past:

- She **rose** from the chair, **walked** up to him, **took** his hand into her own and **marched** off.
- He did not **sleep** at all, **kept awake** the whole night and **dozed off** in the office.
- I **took** the envelop from her, **unfolded** it and **dropped** it on the table.
- **Did** you **meet** Sagar on 1st July as was scheduled earlier?
- **Did** they **go** to the pictures yesterday? (Sometimes specific time in the past is mentioned as shown in the above two cases).

To speak of a state that existed for a while in the past, but is now over:

- I **worked** in air force for ten long years.
- She **did** her **course** here for three weeks.
- They **had** their **schooling** in Delhi.

To speak of actions that happened in the past as a matter of course or routine:

- They **had** their **schooling** in Delhi.
- They **always** quarrelled over trifles.
- He **always** secured first position in the school.
- We **often** debated this issue in the assembly.
- She **regularly** won.
- I **often** played chess with him.

The use of **present perfect** is resorted:

To speak about something that usually happened in the past during a period of time and is not yet over or finished:

- The rain **has been failing** for the last one month.
- The doctor **has not shown** up during the week.
- She **has been coming late** for the last two days.

To speak of a thing happening about which no specific time is mentioned, nor is necessary:

- She **has bought** a new house (it is not known when she bought it).

- They **have cancelled** the tour programme (not known when).
- I **have written** this new book (no specific information about time).
- You **have achieved** a great success (not known when).

To speak of an action completed in the past, but the impact continues to be felt in the present:

- My car is **stolen** (and it is not recovered yet).
- She has **lost** her wallet (and it is still to be found).
- His brother has been **kidnapped** (and police have no clue).

To speak of the duration of an action or state up to the present time using **for/since**:

- I have worked in air force **for** ten years.
- She has been living here **since** 2001.
- **For** how long have you been standing here?
- They have been working **since** morning.

To speak of completion of an action with **already, yet, just** and **ever:**

- The train has just **arrived.**
- They **have** already **booked** their seat.
- **Have** you ever **been** to this temple before?
- **Has** he not **finished** his lunch yet?

The use of **present continuous** or **progressive** is resorted:

To speak of an activity that started in the past and is continuing. This is done with the help of **since** and **for**:

- She has been dancing **since** 5 o'clock in the morning.
- He has been sleeping **for** full eight hours now.
- I have been on this project **since** 2007.
- They have been fighting for their cause **for** a decade now.

Also, to speak of an activity done in the past, but the impact is visible now:

- His shirt is dirty because he **has been repairing** vehicles in the workshop.
- My hands are blood stained because **I have been operating** on a patient.

The **past continuous** or **progressive** is used.

To speak of an action that was in progress at a given time in the past:

- Where **were** you, dad, **when** the lights were off in 1877?
- What **were** you doing **when** Magna Carta was signed?
- Were they **still** playing **when** you left home?
- Where **were** you in 1639 **when** Charles I was executed?

Also, to speak about some action that was already in progress when something else happened thus interrupting the on-going action. Simple past is used for the action that interrupts the action already in progress:

- The priest called when **we were sleeping**.
- The power supply went off when **we were watching** a programme on TV.

The **past perfect** is used:

To speak of an action that happened before another action in the past:

- She has **already been married** before this proposal was sent to her.
- When you called on me, I **had already left** for my office.
- When they reached the airport, the flight **had already taken off**.

The **past perfect continuous or progressive** is used:

To speak of an activity that started at a time further back in the past than something else and such activities are denoted by **for** or **since**:

- I had not been staying long enough when I encountered this problem.
- They had not been doing this before they met the organizer.

Further, to speak about an activity that had a result in a past activity:

- His belly is **full** because **he had been eating** for quite sometime now.
- His linen is **dirty** because **he had been working** in his workshop.

The future

There are many ways of speaking about future.

The future simple is used (*will* with the infinitive):

To speak of a decision we make while we are in the process of speaking:

- It's very hot here. Okay, **let us shift** to a cooler place.
- **You will have** to preserve it.

To speak of what we know or think could possibly happen in the future while we remain ignorant about our own plans or intents:

- The king **will be** anointed tomorrow on attaining the age of twenty-one.
- **Will** you **surmount** this hurdle and scale the height?
- **Will** he **achieve** it, you think?
- This **is** not a tall order.

To speak of requests, offers and promises:

- **Can** you **do** me a favour by getting this job done for me?
- **Will** you **get** me a glass of water?
- **Should** I **do** this for you?
- She **will clear** the hurdle, rest assured.

The present continuous or progressive is used:

To speak of future plans where time is specified:

- I am **going** to quit the bank this July.
- Are you **doing anything** this evening?
- He will **not come** before Monday next.
- Is she **proceeding** to Kolkata tomorrow?

To speak of what we intend to do in future with the use of verb to **be going to** and the infinitive:

- She **is going to make** an overture to him tomorrow.
- I **am going to take up** a new assignment after this one.
- What **are you going to do** after your retirement?
- What **is he proposing to do** after his schooling?

To speak of things that could happen in very near future with the help of **about to** and the infinitive:

- **Go and find** it out expeditiously.

- She **is about to** rise to deliver her speech.
- It **is going to** rain anytime now.
- They **are about to** launch the scheme.

The **present simple** is used to refer to a future time after **as soon as, when, until, before,** etc.:

- Call me **when** you need my help.
- Knock at the door **as soon as** you hear the noise.
- Do not disturb me **until** you have heard from me again.
- You will get to know **before** it is too late.

Also, to speak about future plans which are officially pre-arranged and time schedules finalized or time tables fixed:

- The meeting **starts** at 7 in the morning.
- The school **re-opens** on Monday at 9 sharp.
- The train **leaves** the station at 12 and **reaches** the destination at 6 in the evening.
- They **leave** Pune at 8 in the morning and **reach** Patna at 6 in the evening.

The **future continuous** or **progressive** is used.

To speak of those actions that will continue for a period of time in future:

- She **will be pleading** your case in the court tomorrow.
- I **shall be armed to the teeth** for the battle ahead.
- He **will be guarding** the gate.
- They **will be standing in queue** at the theatre.
- I **will be clearing** the deck for him.

To enquire about somebody's plans/programmes or intentions:

- How long **will** you be **staying** at this place?
- Will she be **staying** back or **returning** to Patna tonight?
- Will you **complete** the work or **leave** for home?

The use of future perfect or future perfect continuous or progressive is resorted:

To speak of the duration of something we will be looking back to at a particular time in future:

- I **shall have completed** ten years in July this year.

- You **will have accomplished** the task in December next year.
- He **will have been teaching** in this school for two years in November.

In order to fully comprehend all aspects of tense in its variegated forms, we have to set them down in a tabular form as under:

Table I

Present				Past			
Present indefinite or simple present	**Present continuous/ progressive**	**Present perfect**	**Present perfect continuous/ progressive**	**Past indefinite or simple past**	**Past continuous/ progressive**	**Past perfect**	**Past perfect continuous progressive**
I play	I am playing	I have played	I have been playing	I played	I was playing	I had played	I had been playing
Future / Future in the Past							
Future indefinite or simple future	**Future continuous/ progressive**	**Future perfect**	**Future perfect continuous/ progressive**	**Future in the past indefinite**	**Future in the past continuous/ progressive**	**Future in the past perfect**	**Future in the past perfect continuous**
I shall play	I shall be playing	I shall have played	I shall have been playing	I should play	I should be playing	I should have played	I should have been playing.

Table II

Tense in active voice

	Present Tense	Past Tense	Future Tense	Future in the Past
Indefinite or Simple	I play	I played	I shall play	I should play
Continuous	I am playing	I was playing	I shall be playing	I should be playing
Perfect	I have played	I had played	I shall have played	I should have played
Perfect Continuous	I have been playing	I had been playing	I shall have been playing	I should have been playing

Tense in passive voice

	Present Tense	Past Tense	Future Tense	Future in the Past
Indefinite	I am asked	I was asked	I shall be asked	I should be asked
Continuous	I am being asked	I was being asked	–	–
Perfect	I have been asked	I had been asked	I shall have been asked	I should have been asked
Perfect Continuous	–	–	–	–

Active Voice (Person)

Present Tense

	Singular	**Plural**
First Person	I see	We see
Second Person	You see	You see
Third Person	He sees	They see

Past Tense

	Singular	**Plural**
First Person	I saw	We saw
Second Person	You saw	You saw
Third Person	He saw	They saw

Future Tense

	Singular	**Plural**
First Person	I shall see	We shall see
Second Person	You will see	You will see
Third Person	He will see	They will see

Passive Voice (Person)

Present Tense

	Singular	**Plural**
First Person	I am seen	We are seen
Second Person	You are seen	You are seen
Third Person	He is seen	They are seen

Past Tense

	Singular	**Plural**
First Person	I was seen	We were seen
Second Person	You were seen	You were seen
Third Person	He was seen	They were seen

Future Tense

	Singular	**Plural**
First Person	I shall be seen	We shall be seen
Second Person	You will be seen	You will be seen

Third Person	He will be seen	They will be seen

In addition to the above, a verb has three forms to express itself in and they are–Present Tense, Past Tense and Past Participle. In the examples that follow we will see how a simple present tense (V1) becomes past tense (V2) and then past participle (V3):

Present tense	**Past tense**	**Past participle**
Arise	arose	arisen
Abide	abode	abode
Bear (produce)	bore	born
Bear (carry)	bore	borne
Beat	beat	beaten
Become	became	become
Behold	beheld	beholden, beheld
Bite	bit	bitten, bit
Bend	bent	bent
Break	broke	broken
Blow	blew	blown
Bid	bade, bid	bidden, bid
Begin	began	begun
Catch	caught	caught
Chide	chid, chided	chid, chidden
Choose	chose	chosen
Close	closed	closed
Cling	clung	clung
Cleave	clove, cleft	cleft, cloven
Climb	climbed, clomb*	climbed
Crow	crowed, crew*	crown*, crowed
Cry	cried	cried
Draw	drew	drawn
Drive	drove	driven
Drink	drank	drunk, drunken#
Dig	dug	dug
Die	died	died
Do	did	done
Eat	ate	eaten
Fall	fell	fallen

Fight	fought	fought
Fling	flung	flung
Fly	flew	flown
Free	freed	freed
Forget	forgot	forgotten
Freeze	froze	frozen
Go, wend	went	gone
Get	got	got, gotten*
Give	gave	given
Grind	ground	ground
Grow	grew	grown
Hide	hid	hid, hidden
Hold	held	held
Know	knew	known
Knit	knit	knit, knitted
Lie	lay, laid	laid, lain
Lie	lied	lied
Lick	licked	licked
Melt	melted	melted
Mellow	mellowed	mellowed
Mow	mowed	mown
Ride	rode	ridden
Ring	rung	rung
Rinse	rinsed	rinsed
Rise	rose	risen
Rot	rotted	rotted, rotten
Rip	ripped	ripped
Rive	rived	riven
Run	ran	run
Saw	sawed	sawn
See	saw	seen
Seethe	seethed	seethed, sodden*
Sew	sewed	sewn
Shake	shook	shaken
Shine	shone	shone
Sing	sang	sung

Sink	sank	sunk, sunken
Show	showed	shown
Sit	sat	sat
Slay	slew	slain
Sling	slung	slung
Slink	slunk	slunk
Smother	smothered	smothered
Sow	sowed	sown
Spin	spun	spun
Spring	sprang, sprung	sprung
Stand	stood	stood
Stick	stuck	stuck
Stink	stank	stunk
Sting	stung	stung
Slide	slid	slid, slidden*
Speak	spoke, spake*	spoken
Steal	stole	stolen
Strike	struck	struck, stricken*
Strive	strove	striven
Swear	swore	sworn
Swell	swelled	swollen
Swim	swam	swum
Swing	swung	swung
Take	took	taken
Tear	tore	torn
Throw	threw	thrown
Tread	trod	trodden, trod
Treat	treated	treated
Threat	threatened	threatened
Unite	united	united
Use	used	used
Volunteer	volunteered	volunteered
Veer	veered	veered
Wash	washed	washed
Wear	wore	worn
Weave	wove	woven

Win	won	won
Wind	wound	wound
Wring	wrung	wrung
Write	wrote	written
Writhe	writhed	writhen, writhed

While the above are the mixed verbs, given below are some of the verbs that take't' to make it to the past tense:

Creep	crept	crept
Weep	wept	wept
Keep	kept	kept
Sleep	slept	slept
Sweep	swept	swept
Dwell	dwelt	dwelt
Burn	burnt	burnt
Deal	dealt	dealt
Dream	dreamt	dreamt
Smell	smelt	smelt
Spell	spelt	spelt
Feel	felt	felt
Kneel	knelt	knelt
Smell	smelt	smelt
Mean	meant	meant
Lean	leant, leaned	leant, leaned
Spill	spilt	spilt
Spoil	spoilt	spoilt

And there are others like these where there is an internal change of vowel:

Bring	brought	brought
Beseech	besought	besought
Seek	sought	sought
Buy	bought	bought
Teach	taught	taught
Catch	caught	caught
Tell	told	told
Sell	sold	sold
Think	thought	thought

There are some other verbs that do not change at all. For instance:

Burst	burst	burst
Cast	cast	cast
Cost	cost	cost
Cut	cut	cut
Put	put	put
Hit	hit	hit
Hurt	hurt	hurt
Let	let	let
Rid	rid	rid
Bet	bet	bet
Thrust	thrust	thrust
Set	set	set
Shed	shed	shed
Shut	shut	shut
Slit	slit	slit
Spit	spit, spat	spit
Split	split	split
Spread	spread	spread
Sweat	sweat	sweat
Quit	quit (quitted)	quit (quitted)
Wed	wed (wedded)	wed (wedded)
Knit	knit (knitted)	knit (knitted)

Then there are some verbs (at least there are nine of them) that end in *d* in the present tense, but as they move to past and past partici ple they shed their *d* and take *t* in lieu with some exceptions. They are:

Bend	bent	bent
Lend	lent	lent
Build	built	built
Send	sent	sent
Rend	rent	rent
Gild	gilt (gilded)	gilt
Gird	girt (girded)	girt
Spend	spent	spent

Wend	went, wended	wended

And yet, there are some verbs that shorten themselves as they move to past and past partici ple. They are:

Bleed	bled	bled
Breed	bred	bred
Feed	fed	fed
Speed	sped	sped
Meet	met	met
Lead	led	led
Read	read#	read#
Light	lit, lighted	lit, lighted
Shoot	shot	shot

* Spake is seldom used

While pronouncing the word, the letter *a* is ignored so that it sounds like *red*.

□

Structure

An important aspect of grammar is STRUCTURE. They are best discussed immediately after dealing with tense and verb. They are as follows:

I. Preparatory= there + verb 'to be' + subject

	There + verb 'to be'	subject *etc.*
1)	There is	a mat on the floor.
2)	There is	a temple near the station.
3)	There is	a stove near the cot.
4)	There was	someone near the gate.
5)	There are	seven days in a week.
6)	There is	lot of water in the tank.

II. To-infinite after adjectives to express emotion or desire.

	Subject + verb	adjective	to-infinitive
1	I shall be	glad	to receive you.
2	We were	delighted	to honour him.
3	He is	frightened	to meet her.
4	My mother is	keen	to visit me.
5	She is	relieved	to see him.
6	The neighbour is	restless	to return.

III. It + verb 'to be' + adjective + of + noun/pronoun + to-infinitive

	It + to be	adjective	of +noun/ pronoun	to-infinitive
1	It is	nice	of you	to come here.
2	It is	horrid	of you	to play dirty tricks.
3	It was	smart	of him	to make it.
4	It was	stupid	of her	to trust him.

5 It was	naïve	of Peter	to make the offer.
6 It was	great	of them	to honour him.

The adjectives that can be thus used in this category are: *clever, intelligent, foolish, kind, nice, generous, smart, polite, wise, brave, considerate, unwise, wrong, cowardly, wicked, silly, careless,* etc.

IV. 'To' infinitive after such adjectives as *difficult, easy, impossible, hard,* etc.

	Subject + verb	**adjective**	**'to' infinitive**
1	The job at hand is	difficult	to perform.
2	The stone is	difficult	to move.
3	The problem is	easy	to solve.
4	The task is	hard	to accomplish.
5	The book is	impossible	to leave unread.
6	It is	pleasant	to walk in this garden.

V. It + be + adjective + 'to' infinitive

	It + be	**adjective**	**'to' infinitive**
1	It is	difficult	to perform the job at hand.
2	It is	easy	to do this sum.
3	It will be	difficult	to teach statistics.
4	It is	uncharitable	to accuse him.
5	It may be	difficult	to attain this objective.
6	It is	cruel	to torture animals.

VI. It + be + no good, etc. + gerundial phrase

	It + be	**gerundial phrase**
1	It is no use	asking for alms here.
2	It is no good	seeking her blessings.
3	It is no use	clamouring for justice.
4	It was no good	talking to him.
5	It has been a pleasure	talking to you.
6	It is worth	reading the book.
7	It was worthwhile	taking part in the debate.

VII. It + to take + me, her, etc. + time phrase + to-infinitive

	It + to take	**time phrase**	**to-infinitive, etc.**
1	It took her	a few minutes	to do the job.
2	It took me	half an hour	to reach the place.
3	It will take you	four days	to make it.

4	It took them	five weeks	to do it.
5	It takes them	a month	to complete the task.
6	It has taken them	two hours	to reach the bus stand.
7	It will take me	one hour	to walk the distance.

VIII. It + be + adjective/noun + noun clause

	It + be	**adjective/noun**	**noun clause**
1	It is	surprising	that she should have treated me like this.
2	It is	unlikely	that it will rain this forenoon.
3	It is	likely	that he will finally return to our fold.
4	It is	doubtful	that he will co-operate with us.
5	It is	probable	that he will surrender before the police.
6	It was	fortunate	that they managed to escape the death-trap.

IX. Too + adjective/adverb + to-infinitive

	Subject + verb	**too + adjective/adverb**	**to-infinitive, etc.**
1	She is	too pre-occupied	to take up this job.
2	I was	too engrossed in my work	to notice him.
3	Her mother is	too weak	to handle the task.
4	I am	too busy	to work for him.
5	He is	too dull	to do this work.
6	She played	too slowly	to make an impact.

X. So + adjective/adverb + that-clause

	Subject + verb	**so + adjective/ adverb**	**that–clause**
1	She is	so pre-occupied	that she cannot take up this job.
2	I was	so engrossed in my work	that I could not notice him.
3	Her mother is	so weak	that she cannot handle the task.
4	I am	so busy	that I cannot work for him.
5	He is	so dull	that he cannot do this work.
6	She played	so slowly	that she could not make an impact.

XI. Adjective/adverb + enough + to-infinitive

	subject + verb	adjective/adverb + enough	to-infinite, etc.
1	He is	intelligent enough	to effectively do this job.
2	She is	belligerent enough	to shout him into submission.
3	You are	clever enough	to overcome this problem.
4	They are	resourceful enough	to get the job done.
5	He ran	fast enough	to beat his adversary.
6	She is	efficient enough	to resolve this technical crisis.
7	The man is	smart enough	to successfully tackle it.

XII. Exclamatory sentences and their patterns

i) What + (adjective+) noun (+ subject + verb)

	What (+adjective+) noun	(subject + verb)
1	What a silly man	(he is)!
2	What a beautiful sight	(it is)!
3	What a great performance	(it was)!
4	What a poor choice	(you made)!
5	What a delicate touch	(it was)!
6	What a pity	(you didn't make it)!
7	What a fool	(he is)!

ii) How + adjective/adverb+subject+verb

	How + adjective/adverb	subject + verb
1	How sweet	she is!
2	How boring	he is!
3	How intelligent	they are!
4	How well	you are looked after!
5	How quietly	he did it!
6	How well	she conducted herself !
7	How serene	the lake is!

□

Conditional Sentences

Some of the conditional statements given below tell us that something will happen if certain conditions are met. It is another matter that the conditions may or may not be met. They are set in three categories in the manner given below:

I. Type 1 conditionals (open conditions with strong possibilities)

If clause simple present	**principal clause will/shall/can/ may infinitive**
1 If I work hard	I will make the grade.
2 If you study hard	you will compete.
3 If it does not rain	I will go today itself.
4 If I find him	I shall ask him for help.
5 If she prepares well	she will win the race.
6 If my father arrives	I will obtain his permission.

II. Type II conditionals (improbable or presumed conditions)

If clause simple past	**principal clause would/should/ might/could+ infinitive**
1 If I worked hard	I would make the grade.
2 If you studied hard	you would compete.
3 If it did not rain	I would go.
4 If I had a sponsor	I could easily make it.
5 If we did it now	it should not be a problem.
6 If she were him	she would not do it.

III. Type III conditionals (unfulfilled conditions)

	If clause past perfect	**principal clause would/should/ could/might+perfect infinitive**
1	If I had worked hard	I would have made the grade.
2	If she had studied hard	she would have competed.
3	If they had tried hard	they would have achieved it.
4	If you had left the dog alone	you would not have been bitten.
5	If you had approached me	you could have been accommodated.
6	If she had tried again	she would have won it.

Conditionals further simplified: sentences with ***if*** are used to express possibilities. As indicated above, there are three conditionals plus a zero conditional explained below–

Conditional one

If clause present tense

Principal or **main clause** future tense

To indicate the consequence of a **possible** action:

If he **does complete the work** this evening, **he will have** our leave to go tonight. (This suggests that there is sufficient time for completion of the job at hand and clear possibility of his being able to go).

Conditional two

If clause simple past

Principal or **main clause** conditional tense

To indicate the consequence of a **hypothetical** action:

If he **did the work** this evening, **he would have** our leave to go tonight. (Though there is time, it is less likely that the work will be completed and he will be able to go, because the chances are he will not be able to do the work).

Conditional three

If clause past perfect

Principal or main clause conditional perfect tense

To indicate the possibility of an action that could have

happened but **did not happen**:

If he **had done the work** this evening, **he would have had** time to go tonight. (It is obvious that he has not been able to do the assigned work. It is, therefore, impossible for him now to go).

Zero conditional

To indicate that something has always been true in the past and expectedly, will be true always because such sentences with **if** express certainty rather than possibility:

If you **freeze** water, it **becomes** ice. (Present simple in both parts of the sentence)

If you **will** strike it hard, it **will** break into pieces. (Future simple in both parts of the sentence)

If you **turned** it upside down, the container always **emptied** itself. (Past simple in both parts of the sentence).

□

Idioms

Every language has phrases or sentences that cannot be understood literally. Even if you know the meaning of all the words in a phrase and understand the grammatical applications thoroughly, the meaning of phrase may still be confusing. Many proverbs, informal phrases, and common sayings offer this kind of problem. A phrase or a sentence of this kind is said to be idiomatic. An idiom is a phrase. Its meaning is at times difficult and at times impossible to guess by looking at the meaning of individual words it contains.

For example, **in the soup** has a literal meaning that is easy to comprehend. It also has a common idiomatic meaning:

My help to him landed me in the soup.
I had not foreseen the dangers ahead.

Here, landed **in the soup** means 'in a bad situation'. Some idioms are imaginative expressions like **too many cooks spoil the broth** (If too many people get involved in a thing, it is likely that it will not be done). Some expressions are so very well known that a part of it is usually left out:

It's pointless to argue with them–
It's the usual story of belling the cat.

Here, it means there is no point in arguing with them because these arguments will lead to no logical conclusion. Or, the lengthy discussion will come to a ridiculous end because no one will be in a position to take the required steps to set things right. We are all familiar with the story of the mice troubled by cat. Their decision to put a bell across the neck of the cat so that they were forewarned came to a naught when someone from among them asked who was going to bell the cat. So, *who will bell the cat* is an idiom suggestive of meaningless discussion.

Given below is a list of some such randomly selected idioms:

A bird in the hand is worth two in the bush. It is a proverb meaning that something you have is always better than something you might have in future.

A fool and his money are soon parted. This refers to a person who uses his money unwisely and loses it.

A friend in need is a friend indeed. This means that a true friend is he who stands by you in your moments of distress. Such a friend is dependable.

Any port in a storm means when in distress, you accept any help that is forthcoming.

A little learning (knowledge) is a dangerous thing. Incomplete knowledge can be embarrassing and harmful.

Absence makes the heart grow fonder. This means that when you are away from a person you love, your love for such a person grows.

Actions speak louder than words. What a person does is more important than what he says he would do.

All that glitters (glisters)* is not gold. This proverb means that many attractive and alluring things have no value.

As good as one's word. Obedient to one's promise; dependable in keeping one's promise.

A rolling stone gathers no moss means if you keep hopping from one place to another, from one job to another, you are unlikely to succeed in life.

A stitch in time saves nine means it is better to immediately attend to a problem before it grows out of control.

At odds means being in opposition to someone or something.

Baptism of fire means a first experience of something usually difficult and unpleasant.

Bank on something means to count on something or to rely on something for support.

Bark up the wrong tree means to make wrong choice; to follow wrong course.

Be a cold fish means to be a person who is distant and unfeeling.

Beauty is in the eyes of the beholder. People see things according to their own perceptions.

Beauty is only skin-deep. How a person looks is less important than his character.

Birds of a feather flock together. People of the same kind are usually found together.

Blood is thicker than water. Family relations are stronger than any other relation.

Born with a silver spoon in your mouth means having rich parents.

Be beside oneself means to be emotionally uncontrolled; to be excited; to be disturbed.

Beggar description means to be impossible to describe well enough to give an accurate picture; to be impossible to do justice to words.

Better safe than sorry means it is wiser to be careful and slow than to be hasty and regret later.

Blessing in disguise means something that turns out to be fortunate and advantageous after seeming to be the opposite at first.

Blow one's own trumpet means to indulge in self-praise: to boast or praise oneself.

Blow hot and cold means to be changeable or uncertain about something.

Blow one's top means to become very angry; to lose one's temper.

Blow the gaff means to reveal some secret, especially to reveal something to the police.

Blow the lid off means to reveal something, especially the wrong doings.

Blow the whistle means to report someone's wrong doings to someone.

Cock a snook at someone means showing of defiance or scorn.

Clutch at straws means to seek something that is difficult to attain or reach; to make a futile attempt at something.

Cloak-and-dagger involves plotting and secrecy.

Cold comfort is no comfort or no consolation at all.

Come a cropper means to have a misfortune; to fail miserably; to fall off a horse.

Come of age means to reach an age when one is old enough to enter into legal contracts.

Come to blows means to fight or quarrel about something.

Cook the books means cheating in book-keeping to show tallying of balances when they are not.

Clear the air means to remove doubts and hostile feelings.

Cut your coat according to your cloth means act within your means.

Curiosity killed the cat means do not try to know or query things that do not concern.

Cut corners means to reduce efforts or expenditures; to do things poorly or incompetently.

Cut loose is to break away from someone or something.

Cut both ways means to affect both sides of an issue in equal measure.

Daddy of them all is the best or the most extreme example of something or someone.

Daily grind is the everyday routine of work.

Damp squib is something that fails to be as successful or exciting as it promised to be.

Dark horse is someone about which very little is known to others (usually associated with horse racing).

Dead and buried is something that is gone for ever.

Desert a sinking ship and leave a sinking ship is to leave a place, a person or a situation when things become unpleasant or difficult.

Die with one's boots on means to die fighting.

Dig in is to get set for a very long session or job.

Discretion is the better part of valour means to avoid danger and not to take unnecessary risks.

Dog-eat-dog is a situation where one has to act ruthlessly in order to survive or succeed.

Dog in the manger is a person who prevents other people from enjoying a thing he himself cannot enjoy. He is a selfish person. It evolved from the story of a dog that did not eat hay, but stayed in the hay-stack so that other animals could be prevented from eating hay.

Don't judge a book by its cover means do not get swayed by external features.

Doubting Thomas is the one who will not easily believe a thing said or done unless strong evidence or proof is adduced.

Down and eat means having no money or means of support.

Down in the dumps means sad and depressed.

Down in the mouth means sad-faced; depressed or unsmiling.

Down the drain means something lost for ever and wasted.

Draw a red herring is to introduce information which diverts attention from the main issue.

Drop a bombshell is to make an announcement that shocks or startles.

Dry run is a rehearsal; an attempt.

Easier said than done means it is easy to talk about a thing, but not easy to actually do it.

Eat humble pie is to act very humbly, especially when one is shown to be wrong.

Eat one's words is to have to take back one's statement or to confess that one's predictions were wrong.

Eat out or dine out is to eat a meal at a restaurant.

Elbow-grease is physical exertion or hard work.

Empty vessels sound much means it is usually the least intelligent and the most ill-informed that are quick to state their opinions.

Enough is enough means that is enough and that there should be no more of it.

Every cloud has a silver lining means every sad or difficult situation has a positive side.

Every dog has its day and every dog has his day means that everyone will get a chance.

Every Tom, Dick and Harry means everyone without discrimination; ordinary people.

Extenuating circumstances means special circumstances which account for an irregular or improper way of doing something.

Face the music means to receive punishment; to accept the unpleasant results of one's own actions.

Face value is the outward appearance; what something appears to be.

Fair-weather friend means someone who is one's friend only when things are rosy or going well and will desert when friend is in distress.

Fall by the way side means to give up and quit before the end of something; not to succeed.

Fall from grace means to cease to be held in favour, especially because of some foolish or wrong action.

Fat chance means small possibilities or very little likelihood.

Feather one's nest is to use power and prestige selfishly to provide for oneself, often illegally and immorally.

Feel the pinch and feel the draught means to have money problems; to experience hardshi ps because of dearth of money.

Fine feathers make fine birds is a proverb that means that one can become attractive by wearing fine and attractive clothes.

Fine kettle of fish means a real mess; an unsatisfactory situation.

Fish in the troubled waters is to involve oneself in a difficult, confused or dangerous situation in order to reap some benefit.

Flash in the pan is something that draws a lot of attention for a very brief period of time.

Flea in one's ears is a severe scolding (usually one receives when one tries to give an unsolicited advice to someone who is not keen to take it).

Flight of fancy is an idea or suggestion that is out of touch with reality or is in the domain of possibility.

Flog a dead horse means to continue to discuss a thing that has long been concluded or all interest in the subject is gone for ever.

Fly-by-night refers to a person or an institution that is not trustworthy.

Fool's paradise is a situation or condition of seeming happiness based on false assumptions not to last long.

Fools rush in where angels fear to tread means people with little experience venture to do things an expert would not dare to do.

Forewarned is forearmed means if you know about a problem beforehand, you get ready to meet and thwart it.

Gain ground means to make progress; to advance; to become more important or popular.

Get a raw deal means to receive unfair or bad treatment.

Get a red face is to blush from embarrassment.

Get a tongue-lashing is to get a severe reprimand or scolding.

Get bogged down is to become stuck with something; to be prevented from progressing further.

Get the boot is to be sent away; to be dismissed from employment; to be kicked out of a place.

Get the blues means to become sad or depressed.

Gird up one's loins is to be ready for something.

Give somebody an inch, he will take a yard is about people who if accommodated will seek to be accommodated more.

Give oneself airs means to act in a superior or conceited way.

Give the devil his due is to give credit even to our enemies when they actually deserve.

Gloss over something is to cover up or conceal an error; to give an appearance of correctness when the thing is wrong.

Go bananas means to go crazy or become silly.

Go haywire is to go wrong; to malfunction.

Go into a tail-spin is when a plane loses control and spins back to the earth, nose first.

Go into orbit is to become very excited; to be in a state of ecstasy.

Go off a tangent means to suddenly swerve in a different direction; to suddenly change one's thought.

Go on a binge is to do too much of something; to do something excessively.

Go the distance is to complete the assigned task by doing all that is required to be done.

Go the whole hog is to do everything possible; to be extravagant.

Go to dogs OR **go to pot** is to deteriorate or to go to ruins.

Go to rack and ruin OR **go to wrack and ruin** means to go to ruins.

Grasp the nettle is to tackle a difficult or unpleasant task with firmness and determination.

Grey area is an area of a subject difficult to categorize for want of clearly defined elements and may have ingredients of other categories.

Grey matter is intelligence; brains or power of thoughts in an individual.

Grin and bear it means to endure something unpleasant with good humour.

Grist to the mill is something which can be put to profitable use.

Hand in glove (with someone) suggests closeness to someone, usually associated with doing something that is improper; say hand in glove in commission of a crime.

Handle someone with kid gloves means to be very careful with a sensitive or a touchy person.

Handsome is as handsome does means that it is very good to be good looking, but good looks alone do not count for much unless one really needs other qualities as well to be regarded as handsome.

Hang by a hair OR **hang by a thread** means to be in an uncertain position; to depend on something very insubstantial.

Hang fire is to delay or wait.

Hang loose means to relax; to remain calm.

Hard nut to crack OR **tough nut to crack** means a difficult person or a thing to deal with.

Have a ball means to have a real enjoyable time.

Have a bee in one's bonnet is to have an idea or a thought remaining in one's mind; to have an obsession.

Have a bone to pick with someone means to have a matter to discuss or sort out with someone.

Have a brush with something means to have a brief contact with something or experience with something, esp. law.

Have feet of clay means to have a defect of character.

Have one's back to the wall means to be in a defensive position.

Have the Midas touch means to have the ability to succeed.

He who hesitates is lost means if you delay doing a thing, the opportunity may slip out of your hand.

He who laughs last laughs longest warns somebody not to be proud of present success; in the end someone else may become successful.

Heads will roll means some people will get into trouble.

Hem and haw OR **hum and haw** means to be evasive and uncertain about something.

Hobson's choice is the choice between taking what is offered and getting nothing at all.

Hoist with one's own petard means to be harmed or disadvantaged by an act that was targeted against someone else. (taken from a line in *Hamlet–She intended to murder her brother but was hoist with her own petard when she ate the poisoned food intended for him*).

Hold one's piece means to remain silent and calm.

Hold out the olive branch is to offer to end a dispute and be friendly; to offer reconciliation.

Hold the fort means to oversee and look after a place such as a business outlet or home.

Hole-in-corner OR **hole-in-the-corner** means something dishonest and secret; secretive.

Hot under the collar means very angry.

Hue and cry is a loud public protest.

Hush money means money paid by way of a bribe; bribery.

Ignorance is bliss means if you do not know about a thing, you do not worry about it.

If you can't beat them, join them. If you cannot stop a thing from happening, it is better to become part of that thing and enjoy the benefits that accrue therefrom.

In a quandary means to be in a state of confusion; uncertain about what to do.

In apple-pie order means to be in very good order; very well organized.

In cahoots with someone means in conspiracy with someone; in league with someone.
In fine feather means to be in good humour; in good health.
In one's own backyard means very close to someone.
In the pink (of condition) is suggestive of very good health and condition both emotionally and physically.
It never rains but it pours means that a lot of bad things tend to happen at the same time.
It's folly to be wise where ignorance is bliss means do not flaunt your knowledge amongst the fools.
Jack of all trades is someone who can do several different things without being a specialist in one job.
Jekyll and Hyde means a person with both good and evil personified in one person.
Jockey for position means to try to push or manoeuvre one's way into an advantageous position at the cost of others.
Jump the gun is to start before the starting signal.
Keep a stiff upper lip means to remain cool and unmoved even in the moments of unsettling events.
Keep a straight face means to keep one's face free from expressions of joy.
Keep abreast (of something) OR **be abreast (of something)** means to remain informed about things or to keep up with the times.
Keep cool means stay calm and unruffled.
Keep late hours means to stay up or stay out until very late.
Keep on an even keel means to remain cool and calm.
Kill the goose that laid the golden egg is to say about the destruction of the source of one's good fortune.
Kill time is to waste time.
Kill two birds with one stone is to solve two problems with one solution.
Kiss and make up is to forgive someone and be friends again.
Know which side one's bread is buttered on is to know what is most advantageous for one.
Laid back means to be relaxed and at ease.

Lame duck is someone or something that is helpless, useless and inefficient.

Lash out is to threaten or attack someone physically or verbally.

Last but not the least means last in sequence, but not in importance.

Least said the soonest mended means the less one says the less harm one does.

Leave a lot to be desired means to be inadequate or to be lacking in something important.

Leave no stone unturned means to search in all possible places or directions.

Leave someone high and dry means to leave someone unsupported to fend for himself.

Left, right and centre means everywhere; to an excessive extent.

Let sleeping dogs lie means that one should not search for trouble.

Let the cat out of the bag OR **spill the beans** means to reveal a secret or a surprise by accident.

Lightening never strikes twice (in the same place) means it is highly unlikely that the same misfortune will occur again in the same set of circumstances or to the same people.

Likes of someone means the type of person someone is; anyone like someone.

Life is life everywhere means a life can be usefully lived irrespective of the place.

Line one's own pockets means to make money for oneself in a greedy or dishonest manner.

Live in an ivory tower means to remain aloof or separated from the realities of life around.

Lock, stock, and barrel means everything.

Loom large means to be of great importance, especially when referring to a possible problem, danger or threat.

Maiden speech means first public speech.

Maiden voyage is the first voyage of a ship or boat.

Make a fast buck means to make money with little effort.

Make hay while the sun shines means make best possible use of the available opportunities.

Make a mountain out of a molehill is to make a major issue out of a minor one; to exaggerate the importance of something.

Make a point means to state an item of importance.

Make both ends meet is to manage to live on a small amount of money.

Make mincemeat of someone means to comprehensively defeat someone; to defeat completely.

Make mischief means to cause trouble.

Make oneself conspicuous means to attract attention to one's ownself.

Make someone eat crow is to make someone to retract a statement or admit an error.

Meet one's Waterloo is to meet one's final and insurmountable challenge.

Melt in one's mouth is to taste very good.

Method in one's madness means purpose in what one is doing (taken from *Hamlet* of *Shakespeare*).

Millstone about one's neck means a continual burden or handicap.

Neither fish nor fowl means not any recognizable thing.

Neither here nor there means of no consequence or meaning; irrelevant and immaterial.

Never say die means never give up hope.

New lease on life means a renewed and revitalized outlook on life.

Nine days' wonder means a thing that is of interest to people only for a short period.

Nip something in the bud is to put an end to something at an early stage.

No holds barred means with no restraints.

No ifs and buts about it means absolutely no discussion, dissension or doubt about something.

No love lost means no friendship wasted between someone and someone else because they are enemies.

None the wiser means not knowing any more.

Nothing to write home about means nothing exciting or of interest.

Nothing ventured, nothing gained means you cannot achieve anything if you do not try.

Null and void is something that is cancelled, worthless.

Nuts and bolts means the basic facts about something.

One man's meat is another man's poison means what one person may like very much may not be to the liking of the other man.

One swallow does not make a summer means a small indicator that something is happening or will happen in future should not be taken too seriously, for the situation could change.

Odd man out means an unusual or atypical person or a thing.

Odour of sanctity is an atmosphere of excessive holiness or piety (meant derogatively).

Off the beaten track means in an unfamiliar place; on a route which is not usually taken.

Old hand at doing something means someone who is experienced at doing something.

On a fool's errand means involved in a useless journey or task or pursuit.

On cloud nine means very happy (informal).

On edge means nervous.

On hold means something kept in abeyance; temporarily halted.

On one's guard means cautious, alert and vigilant.

On one's own means by one's own self.

On the air means broadcasting a radio or television programme.

On the horns of a dilemma means having to decide between two things or people.

On the mend means getting well, healing (informal).

On the spur of the moment means suddenly, spontaneously.

Out of the woods means getting past a critical phase; no longer at risk.

Out of thin air means out of nowhere; out of nothing (informal).

Out on a limb means in a difficult or dangerous position; taking a chance or a risk.

Pack a punch means to provide a burst of energy, power or excitement.

Pack up means to stop working or functioning. This is both an idiom and a verbal phrase.

Pain in the neck is a bother; an annoyance.

Part company means to sever relationship or to separate from someone or something.

Parting of the ways also means parting of relationship or going separate ways.

Partake of something means taking of something; eating or drinking something.

Pass on OR **pass away** is a euphemism for *death*. Examples: when you *pass on*, what do you care for celebrations! My father *passed away* last week.

Pass muster means to measure up to something or to a required standard.

Pass the buck means to shift the blame on someone else.

Pass the time means to while away one's time or just to fill up time by doing something.

Pastures new means to find some other outlet or fresh fields or a new vocation.

Pave the way is to prepare for something or to facilitate for someone or something.

Pay lip-service means to express solidarity, loyalty, or support for someone or something without sincerity.

Perish the thought OR **banish the thought** means to caution one against even considering certain things.

Pick holes in something means severely criticise; to find fault with or fallacies in arguments.

Piece together means to assemble something from pieces, parts or bits.

Pigs might fly means to suggest something that is not going to happen; something that is highly unlikely to happen.

Pile up means to accumulate or to grow into a pile or adding to pending works.

Pinch and scrape means to survive on very little money in order to save money.

Pipped at the post means beaten at the very end of a competition or a race; defeated in an activity at the very last moment.

Play havoc means to cause a lot of damage to something; to destroy something.

Play to the gallery means to play act in order to draw attention and approval of the lower elements in the audience.

Poetic justice is the chance or appropriate receiving of reward or punishment by those who deserved it.

Put a brave face on it means trying to appear happy or satisfied when faced with adversity or misfortune; and **put up a brave front** means to appear to be brave even when one is not.

Put in an appearance means to make a brief appearance somewhere for the sake of appearance.

Put on an act is a pretentious act of being something one is not.

Put on airs is to act superior.

Put on weight is to gain in weight, to grow obese.

Put best foot forward is to try to do one's best; to make the best attempt possible to make best possible impression.

Put on the back burner means to delay or postpone an action in order to put something on hold.

Queer someone's pitch is to upset or ruin someone's arrangements or designs or chances.

Quick on the uptake means quick to understand something.

Race against time is to hurry to achieve something by a definite time or to hurry to beat a deadline.

Rack one's brain means to try hard to think of something.

Rain cats and dogs means to rain in torrents or hard.

Rake something up is to uncover something unpleasant and remind people about it.

Ramble on is to talk aimlessly about something.

Rank and file means regular soldiers, not the officers.

Rant and rave is to shout angrily and wildly.

Rap knuckles means to rebuke or punish someone.

Raring to go means one is extremely keen to act or do something.

Read between the lines means to infer something from something.

Rear its ugly head means sudden appearance of something unpleasant that had remained hidden for quite some time.

Red herring is a piece of information introduced to draw one away from the truth or real fact of a situation. (These days companies selling IPOs refer buyers to a document called red herring so that they could get to know about what is on offer). A red herring was actually a type of strong-smelling smoked fish used for misleading the hunting dogs to put them off the scent.

Red tape is over-reliance on the wording and details of rules and regulations, especially by governments and public departments.

Rest on one's laurels means to enjoy one's success and not attempt fresh successes.

Return the compliment means to pay a compliment to someone who has paid you a compliment.

Return the favour means to do a good turn to someone who has done you a good deed.

Ride roughshod over something or someone means to treat someone or something with disdain or contempt or scorn.

Ring in the New Year means to celebrate the advent of the New Year at midnight on 31st December.

Ring true means to sound or seem true or likely to be true.

Rise to the occasion suggests you are ready to meet the challenge of an event.

Rob Peter to pay Paul means to take from one person to give to another person.

Rock the boat means to cause trouble or to disturb a situation otherwise stable and quiet.

Rome wasn't built in a day means that a quality thing takes time to fructify or important things don't happen overnight.

Root and branch means completely or entirely. For instance, the system calls for overhauling root and branch.

Ruffle someone's feathers means to annoy or upset someone.

Rule the roost means to be the boss or manager, especially at home.

Run of the mill means common or average; typical.

Run riot OR **run wild** means to get out of control.

Share and share alike means everyone should share things equally and in fair way.

Seamy side of life means the unpleasant or roughest part of one's life.

Second to none means better than anyone or anything else.

See red means to be angry.

See the light at the end of the tunnel means to hope for the end to one's miseries after a prolonged period of time.

See the writing on the walls is to know something unpleasant or disastrous is in store or is going to happen.

Separate the grain from the chaff means setting apart what is of value from what is useless.

Set sail means to depart in a boat for a new destination.

Set forth means to start out on something.

Set off (for somewhere) OR **set out** (for somewhere) means to begin a journey to a place.

Sink or swim means fail or succeed.

Silence is golden means it is often best not to say anything.

Sitting on a powder keg means to be in a risky or explosive situation; to be placed in a situation where something deadly or dangerous may occur.

Slanging match is an angry argument in which both parties are rude to each other.

Slap in the face is an insult; an act that causes discomfort or disappointment.

Slice of the cake is a share of something.

Small fry is an insignificant person or unimportant people or things.

Smear campaign is a campaign aimed at damaging someone's reputation by making accusations and spreading rumours.

Snake in the grass is a low and deceitful person.

Spick and span is something very clean.

Spot on is exactly right or accurate.

Stand to reason means to seem reasonable; that which can stand the scrutiny of logical evaluation.

Stick out like a sore thumb means to be very unsightly or prominent; to be very obvious.

Still waters run deep means a seemingly quiet and reticent person may surprise you with his knowledge and profundity of feelings.

Straw in the wind is an indication or a hint of what might happen in the future.

Strike a bargain means to reach an agreement on a price or something.

Strike a chord is to cause someone to remember; to be familiar or to remind someone of familiarity.

Strike it rich means acquiring sudden wealth.

Stroke of luck is a bit of luck; a lucky happening.

The pot calling the kettle black means you should not criticise someone for the faults you too have, perhaps in greater measure.

The grass is always greener on the other side means that some people are never happy with their own lot and feel the other people are better off.

There's many a slip betwixt (between) cup and lips means you cannot be sure about anything unless it has actually happened, for things could easily go wrong.

The proof of the pudding is in the eating means you can judge the efficacy of a thing only if you have tried it.

Tail wagging the dog means a situation where a small or minor part is controlling the whole thing.

Take heart means to be brave; to have courage.

Take heed is to take notice; to pay attention; to be careful.

Take to task means to scold or reprimand.

Take the floor means to stand up and address the audience.

Talk of the town means the subject of gossip.

Talk shop means to talk business or about business matters.

Talk turkey is to talk business; to talk frankly.

Talking-shop is a place or meeting where things are discussed, no action is taken.

Teething troubles means difficulties and problems experienced in the early stages of a project or work.

The plot thickens means things are becoming more complicated or interesting.

The spirit is willing but the flesh is weak is a biblical reference which means though one is willing to do a thing, one is constrained by physical handicaps.

Throw in the towel means to give up or to surrender.

To the victorious belong the spoils is a proverb that means that the winner takes it all: people and property of the vanquished.

Tongue-in-cheek is simply insincere.

Turn over a new leaf means to start a thing all over again.

Turn turtle means to go upside down.

Twiddle one's thumb means to fill up time by playing with one's fingers.

Two's company, three's a crowd means while two people may like to be together, the presence of a third is a nuisance or annoying.

Under a cloud means to be suspected of having done something.

Up a blind alley means at a dead end; on a route that leads nowhere.

Up a gum-tree means being in a difficult situation and difficult to get out of it.

Up and about means healthy and moving about–not sick in bed.

Up-and-coming means progressing well; set to succeed or prosper.

Up and doing means active and lively,

Up for grabs means available for taking by anyone.

Upper crust means the higher levels of society; the upper class.

Ups and downs means good fortunes and bad fortunes; highs and lows of life.

Upset the applecart means to spoil or ruin something.

Used to someone or something is accustomed to someone or something.

Vanish into thin air means to disappear without a trace.

Variety is the spice of life means that differences and changes are the essential elements of life.

Vexed question means a difficult problem about which there is a lot of discussion without leading to a logical and satisfactory solution.

Vicious circle means a situation wherein solution of one problem leads to second problem, and solution of second problem brings it back to the first problem.

Waiting in the wings means readiness to do something, especially to take over someone else's position or job.

Walk a tightrope refers to a situation that demands utmost carefulness and caution.

Walk on air means to be in a state of extreme happiness; to be euphoric or to be ecstatic.

Walls have ears means we may be overheard.

Warm up means to become lively.

Warts and all means including all the faults and disadvantages.

Waste not, want not means if one does not waste anything, one will never be short of anything.

Water under the bridge means something past and forgotten.

Ways and means is suggestive of methods, often secret or underhanded, of doing or obtaining something.

Wear one's heart on one's sleeves OR **have one's heart on one's sleeves** means habitual display of one's feelings and emotions openly, instead of keeping them private.

Wear out one's welcome means to overstay or to visit too often.

Weasel out means to get out or slide out of something, especially from a gathering of some kind.

Week in, week out means every week, week after week doing the same thing and getting tired and bored therefrom.

Weep buckets means to weep a great many tears.

Weigh one's words means to be careful and choosy about the words one chose while speaking.

Wet blanket is a depressing or a dull person who spoils other people's enjoyment.

What is sauce for the goose is sauce for the gander means what is appropriate for one is equally appropriate for the other.

What price something? is an informal way of enquiring about the value of something.

What with is because.

Wheeling and dealing means taking part in clever though occasionally dishonest and immoral business deals.

Wheels within wheels is suggestive of circumstances, often secret or personal, impacting each leading to confusing and complicated situation.

When in Rome do as the Romans do is a proverb that means that one should behave in the same way as the locals behave.

Where there's a will there's a way means that one can do a thing if one has the inclination to do that.

Where there's smoke there's fire OR **there's no smoke without fire** means that some evidence of a problem indicates that there really is a problem.

Why keep a dog and bark yourself. This means if there is somebody for doing a work, there is no point doing it yourself.

Wide of the mark means far from the target.

Wild-goose chase is a futile pursuit; a worthless hunt or chase.

Win by a whisker OR **win by a nose** means to win by the slightest amount of difference. For instance, *he lost it by a whisker and she won the race of her life, but winning by a nose.*

Window-dressing is a way of showing off one's wares to impress others. This idiom is commonly used to describe the efforts of banks and commercial organizations to show achievement of various targets/budgets by jacking up figures and data.

Window-shopping means the habit or practice of looking at goods in shop-windows without actually intending to buy them.

Wise after the event means becoming knowledgeable about how a situation should have been tackled only after the event has passed.

Wishful thinking is believing that something is true or that something will happen just because one wishes it to happen or wishes it to be true.

With a heavy heart means sadly.

With a vengeance means with vigour; energetically as if one were angry.

With flying colours means doing a thing easily and excellently.

With no strings attached OR **without any strings attached** means unconditional; without any obligations.

Without rhyme or reason means without purpose, order, or reason.

Wolf in sheep's clothing is someone dangerous or ruthless masquerading as kind and gentle.

Wool-gathering is day dreaming.

Year in, year out means year after year, all year long. See also, week in, week out.

Zero hour is a crucial moment when something momentous is to begin.

Zero in on something OR **zoom in on something** means to focus or aim directly on something.

Zonk out is a slang that means to fall asleep or to pass out.

*Aristotle in 4th century BC, Chaucer in 14th century, and Shakespeare in 16th century had used this idiom as *all that glisters is not gold.* It was John Dryden in 1687 in *The Hind and the Panther* that this idiom was used in its present form for the first time and it has continued to be so used ever since.

□

Correct Uses of Prepositions

These are easy to remember prepositional uses. All you need to do is to read them aloud a number of times as they settle in your mind.

Nouns followed by prepositions:-

Ability *for* or *in* something
Abhorrence *of* ingratitude
Abstinence *from* wine
Abundance *of* wealth
Access *to* an authority or an office
Accusation *of* theft
Acquaintance *with* a person or a thing
Adaptation *to* something
Adherence *to* a plan/cause/princi ple
Admission *to* an office/class or *to* a person
Admission *into* a place
Affection *for* a person
Affinity *between* two things
Affinity *with* something
Allegiance *to* a person or *to* an institution
Alliance *with* a person or state
Allusion *to* something or some event
Alternative *to* a plan
Ambition *for* distinction
Amends *for* some faults
Analogy *of* one thing with another

Analogy *between* two things
Animosity *against* a person
Annexation *to* some state or kingdom
Antidote *to* some person
Antidote *against* infection
Anti pathy *to* some animal or some taste
Anxiety *for* one's safety and security
Apology *for* some fault
Appetite *for* food
Application *to* books
Application *for* job
Apprehension *of* danger
Approach *to* anything
Aptitude *for* science
Arrival *at* a place or arrival *in* a country
Ascendancy *over* a person
Aspiration *for* or *after* fame/wealth
Assault *on* a person
Assent *to* a bill or an opinion
Assurance *of* help
Atonement *for* sin
Attachment *to* a person or thing
Attack *on* a place
Attendance *on* a person or attendance *at* a place
Attention *to* study or details
Attraction *to* or *towards* a person or thing
Authority *over* a person or authority *on* a subject
Aversion *to* a thing or person
Ban *on* (a thing)
Ban *from* (a place)
Bargain *with* a person
Bargain *for* a thing
Betrayal *of* a secret
Bias *towards* a thing
Bias *against* a person
Blasphemy *against* (a religious tenet)

Blindness *to* one's fault
Care *for* safety
Care *of* books
Cause *for* anxiety
Cause *of* action/trouble
Caution *against* mistakes
Certainty *about* a matter
Charge *of* murder
Charge *with* murder (verb)
Claim *on* or *against* someone
Claim *to* something
Cloak *for* vice
Cohesion *between, among* things, groups
Collusion *with* a person
Comment *on* a thing
Comment *about* another person
Comment *to* a person
Commerce *with* a country
Comparison *with* a person or thing
Compassion *for* a person
Compensation *for* a loss
Competition *with* a person
Competition *for* a thing
Complaint *against* a person
Complaint *about* a thing
Compliance *with* a request
Complicity *in* a crime
Concession *to* a demand
Concurrence *with* a person
Concurrence *in* a proposal
Condemnation *to* death
Condolence *with* a person
Confidence *in* a person
Conformity *with* any one's views
Conformity *to* a rule
Congruence *with* a standard

Connection *with* a person or a thing
Connivance *at* anyone's faults
Consciousness *of* life
Consideration *of* a thing
Consideration *for* a person
Contact *with* something
Contempt *for* a person
Contemporary *of* a person
Contrast *to* a person or thing
(In) contrast *with* a person or thing
Contribution *to* a fund
Contribution *towards* a cause or project
Control *over* a thing or person
Controversy *on* or *about* something
Controversy *with* a person
Conversation *with* a person
Convergence *to* a point
Conviction *of* guilt
Copartner *with* a person
Copartner *in* something
Copy *from* nature or person
Correspondence *with* a person
Correspondence *to* a thing
Craving *for* anything (appreciation)
Decision *on* some case
Decision *of* a dispute
Degradation *from* rank
Delight *in* a thing or a person
Deliverance *from* death
Dependence *on* a person or thing
Descent *from* ancestors
Desire *for* wealth
Deviation *from* rule
Digression *from* a subject
Dexterity *in* doing something
Disagreement *with* a plan or person

Discouragement *to* a person
Disgrace *to* a person
Disgust *at* something
Dislike *to* a thing or person
Distaste *for* a thing or person
Dissent *from* a proposal
Distrust *of* a person or thing
Doubt *about* or *of* a thing
Drawbacks *to* success
Duty *to* a person or country
Eagerness *for* recognition
Eminence *in* painting
Encroachment *on* one's rights
Economy *of* time
Endeavour *after* happiness
Endurance *of* pain
Engagement *with* a person
Engagement *in* a job
Enmity *with* a person
Entrance *into* a public place
Envy *at* another's success
Equality *with* a person
Escape *from* work
Esteem *for* a person
Estrangement *from* a person
Evasion *of* a system
Exception *to* a rule
Excerpt *from* book
Exemption *from* duty
Experience *of* a thing
Experience *in* doing something
Exposure *to* risk
Failure *of* a scheme
Failure *of* a person
Faith *in* something or person
Familiarity *with* a person or thing

Fine *for* an offence
Fitness *for* some job
Fondness *for* a thing or person
Freedom *of* action
Freedom *from* care
Freedom *at* midnight
Glance *at* a thing or person
Glance *over* a surface
Gratitude *to* a person
Gratitude *for* a favour
Greediness *for* or *after* a thing
Grief *at* an event
Grief *for* a person
Harmony *with* a thing
Hatred *for* or *of* a person
Hatred *of* a thing
Hegemony *over* rivals
Hegemony *in* a region, a field
Heir *to* property
Heir *of* a person
Hindrance *to* a thing
Hint *at* some reward
Hope *for* or *of* better luck
Hostility *to* a person
Hospitality *to* a person
Identity *with* a person or thing
Immersion *into* water
Impatience *with* a person
Impatience *with, at, about* a situation
Impediment *to* progress
Implication *in* a case
Imputation *of* guilt
Imputation *against* someone
Imprecations *on* someone
Imprecations *of* mob
Incentive *to* industry

Inclination *for* work
Inclination *to* study
Indifference *to* person or thing
Indulgence *to* a person
Indulgence *in* wine and luxury
Inference *from* facts or data
Infliction *of* punishment
Influence *over* a person
Inquiry *into* incidents or circumstances
Inkling *of* a thing
Insight *into* something
Intercourse *with* a person
Interest *in* a thing or subject
Interest *with* a person
Interference *with* a man's work
Interview *with* a person
Intimacy *with* a person
Intrusion *into* one's privacy
Invectives *against* a person
Invitation *to* a dinner
Joy *in* good fortune
Judge *of* a matter
Jurisdiction *over* a state
Jurisdiction *in* a law suit
Justification *for* crime
Justification *of* crime
Key *to* success or a mystery
Lax *in* attitude
Laxity *in* morals
Leisure *for* pleasure
Leniency *to* bad elements
Likeness *to* a person
Liking *for* a person
Limit *to* a man's prowess
Longing *for* or *after* a thing
Lust *for* money

Love *of* lucre
Malice *against* or *towards* a person
Margin *for* error
Martyr *for* a cause
Martyr *to* concussion
Mastery *of* a skill
Mastery *over* people
Match *for* a person
Menace *to* public order
Necessity *of* life
Necessity *for* something
Need *of* assistance
Negligence *of* duty
Neglect *of* duty
Neglect *in* executing a thing
Nerve *for* fight
Nomination *to* a post
Nomination *of* a person
Obedience *to* orders
Objection *to* a proposal
Obligation *to* a person
Obstruction *to* free movement of traffic
Offence *against* state
Offence *at* something done
Offset *to* a loss
Opportunity *for* action
Opposition *to* a person
Order *for* or *against* doing something
Partiality *for* flatterers
Partnership *in* a thing
Partnership *with* a person
Passion *for* something
Penance *for* some fault
Penetration *into* something
Persistence *in* an attempt
Piety *towards* God

Pity *for* the poor
Postscript *to* a letter
Precaution *against* disease
Predilection *for* a thing or person
Preface *to* a book
Preference *for* one thing
Preference *to* another thing
Prejudice *against* a person
Preparation *for* examination
Pretension *to* learning
Pretext *for* intervention
Pride *in* something
Prides herself *on* her riches
Proficiency *in* English
Profit *to* the buyer
Prohibition *against* something
Proneness *to* dishonesty
Propensity *to* do a thing
Provocation *to* or *for* an action
Qualification *for* a post
Quarrel *between* two persons
Quarrel *with* another person
Readiness *for* a journey
Readiness *to* do a job
Reason *for* a thing
Reason *against* something
Receptacle *for* something
Reference *to* a person or an event
Regard *for* something
Regret *for* something
Relation *of* one thing to another
Relation *between* two persons or things
Relation *with* a person
Relevancy *to* a question
Remedy *for* or *against* some ailment
Remonstrance *with* a person

Remonstrance *against* conduct
Remorse *for* a sinful act
Repentance *for* sin
Repugnance *to* someone's wishes or desire
Reputation *for* honesty
Request *for* a thing
Resignation *to* fate
Resemblance *to* a person
Resistance *to* injustice
Respect *for* a man or an office
Respite *from* sufferings
Responsibility *to* the state
Responsibility *for* action
Reverence *for* age
Rivalry *with* a person
Sanction *for* misconduct
Sanction *of* a sponsoring body
Sanction *to* a person, an event
Satire *against* follies
Satisfaction *for* something
Satisfaction *of* having done a good job
Search *for* or *after* wealth
Sequel *to* an event
Shame *at* or *for* a fault
Share *of* a thing
Share *with* a person
(A) Slave *to* avarice
(The) slave *of* avarice
Slur *on* character
Sorrow *for* misfortune
Stain *on* character
Stickler *to* rules
Stickler *for* trifles
Submission *to* authority
Subscription *to* a fund
Subsistence *on* pittance

Succession *to* an estate
Supplement *to* something
Surety *for* a person
Suspicion *of* intents
Sympathy *with* or *for* the poor
Taste *for* hard work (preference or personal liking)
Taste *of* hard work (experience)
Temptation *to* evil
Tenacity *of* purpose
Testimony *to* a character
Testimony *against* a character
Title *to* a property
Traitor *to* one's own country
Treatise *on* literature
Trespass *against* the law of the land
Trust *in* one's ability
Umbrage *at* one's behaviour
(In) unison *with* one's character
(She has no) use *for* that
(What is the) use *of* that?
(There is no) use *in* that
(At) variance *with* a person
Victim *to* hooliganism
Victim *of* oppression
Victory *over* poverty
Want *of* money
Warrant *for* one's arrest
Witness *to* an event
Witness *of* a crime
Wonder *at* indifference
Yearning *for* riches
Yen *for* money
Zeal *for* doing something
Zest *for* life

Participles and Adjectives followed by Prepositions:-

Abandoned *to* fate
Abhorrent *to* feelings
Abounding *in* or *with* muck
Absolved *of* a charge
Absorbed *in* prayers
Accessible *to* all
Accessory *to* an act of crime
Accompanied *by* (not with) [something else]
Accomplished *in* a magical art
Accountable *to* the people
Accountable *for* a thing
Accruing *to* a person *from* a thing or two
Accused *of* theft
Accustomed *to* hard labour
Acquainted *with* a person
Acquitted *of* a charge
Adapted *to* new environment
Addicted *to* wine
Adequate *to* his needs
Adjacent *to* a place
Adverse *to* one's interest
Affectionate *to* a person
Afflicted *with* grief
Afraid *of* disease
Agreeable *to* a thing
Alarmed *at* a rumour
Alien *to* his traditions
Alienated *from* the family
Alive *to* a problem
Allied *to* a party
Allied *with* a person or country
Amazed *at* something
Ambitious *of* success
Amenable *to* ideas
Amused *at* a joke

Analogous *to* a thing
Angry *at* a thing
Angry *with* a person
Annoyed *at* a thing
Annoyed *with* a person
Answerable *to* someone
Answerable *for* conduct
Anxious *about* the consequences
Anxious *for* safety
Appalled *at* the prospects
Applicable *to* a case
Apprehensive *of* danger
Apprised *of* facts
Appropriate *to* an occasion
Apt *for* a purpose
Apt *in* accounting
Ashamed *of* misconduct
Assessed *at* a low price
Assiduous *in* his methods
Associated *with* a person
Associated *in* a project
Assured *of* assistance
Astonished *at* her behaviour
Astonishing *to* a person
Averse *to* doing a thing
Aware *of* limitations
Backward *in* his approach
Based *on* principles
Based *in* a place, a field of study
Bent *on* or *upon* doing a thing
Betrayed *to* the enemy
Betrayed *into* the hands of an enemy
Blessed *with* fortune
Binding *on* (not *upon*) a person
Blind *to* one's own fault
Blind *of* one eye

Born *of* rich parents
Born *in* Amsterdam
Bound *by* contract
Bound *for* London
Bound *in* honour
Busy *with* tasks at hand
Capable *of* doing a thing
Careful *about* appearance
Careful *of* belongings
Cautious *of* pitfalls
Certain *of* success
Characteristic *of* a person
Characterized *by* a thing
Charged *to* someone's care
Charged *with* a crime
Clamorous *for* improved service conditions
Clamorous *against* faulty system
Clear *of* accusation
Close *to* a person or thing
Clumsy *at* work
Cognizant *of* an emerging situation
Collateral *with* something else
Commemorative *of* a victory
Commensurate *with* qualifications and experiences
Committed *to* something
Comparable *to* something
Compatible *with* one's temperament
Competent *for* something
Complaisant *to* a person
Composed *of* a material
Compounded *with* something
Condemned *to* life imprisonment
Confident *of* success
Conscious *of* shortcomings
Consistent *with* honesty
Conspicuous *with* diligence

Contiguous *to*, *with* another place
Contemporary *with* another event
Contingent *on* (not *upon*) something
Contrary *to* rules
Contrasted *with* something unrelated
Conversant *with*, *in* a field of study
Convicted *of* a crime
Convinced *of* a fact
Convulsed *with* anger
Covetous *of* others, possessions
Cured *of* a disease
Customary *for* him/her
Deaf *to* pleas/entreaties
Deficient *in* style
Defrauded *of* savings
Deleterious *to* health
Delighted *with* victory
Dependent *on* a person or thing
Depleted *of* stock
Deprived *of* food and money
Derogatory *to* reputation
Deserving *of* praise
Descri ptive *of* a house
Desirous *of* riches
Destined *for* success
Desponded *of* wealth
Detrimental *to* health or interest
Devoid *of* mental alacrity
Dexterous *in* or *at* doing a thing
Different *from* others
Diffident *of* success
Diligent *in* efforts
Disappointed *of* a thing
Disappointed *in* a thing done
Disappointed *with* a person
Disastrous *to* a person

Disgusted *with* a thing or person
Disgusted *at* a person
Dismayed *at* an outcome
Displeased *with* a person
Disqualified *for* a post
Disqualified *from* competing
Dissimilar *to* (not *from*)
Distinct *from* something else
Distracted *with* pain
Divested *of* profit
Doubtful *or* dubious of success
Dull *of* understanding
Eager *for* appreciation
Eager *in* pursuit of something
Earnest *in* efforts
Effective *for* a purpose
Eligible *for* employment
Eminent *for* his munificence
Empty *of* its contents
Enamoured *of* (not *with*) a thing
Endeared *to* all
Endowed *with* prowess
Endowed *with* natural ability
Engaged *to* a person
Engaged *in* a job
Engraved *on* the wood
Enraged *at* something
Entailed *on* a person
Entangled *on* a plot
Entitled *to* justice
Enveloped *in* cloud
Envious *of* one's success
Equal *to* the task
Essential *to* happiness
Estranged *from* wife
Even *with* an adversary

Exempt or exempted *from* tax
Exonerated *from* blame
Exposed *to* danger
Expressive *of* feelings
Faithful *to* employer
False *to* friends
False *of* intents
Familiar *to* a place or person
Familiar *with* a language or situation
Famous *for* his artistry
Fascinated *to* a thing
Fascinated *with* a person or thing
Fatal *to* one's prospects
Fatigued *with* traveling
Fearful *of* consequences
Fertile *in* resources
Fit *for* a position
Fond *of* music
Founded *on* facts
Fraught *with* risk
Free *from* trouble
Full *of* promise or possibilities
Gifted *with* natural abilities
Glad *of* assistance received
Glad *at* success
Glad *to* be of use
Good *for* nothing
Good *at* sports
Grateful *for* assistance received
Greedy *of* or *after* riches
Guilty *of* theft
Gulled *of* one's wealth
Hardened *to* misfortune
Healed *of* disease
Heedless *of* consequences
Held *in* high esteem

Honest *in* dealings
Hopeful *of* success
Horrified *at* the prospects
Hostile *to* my interests
Hungry *after* wealth
Hurtful *to* health
Ignorant *of* rules
Ill *with* fever
Illustrative *of* a mandate
Imbued *with* confidence
Identical *with, to* something else
Imitative *of* another person
Immaterial *to* the subject under discussion
Immersed *in* thought
Impatient *for* worldly success
Impatient *at* an event
Impatient *of* censure
Imperative *on* a person
Impertinent *to* the boss
Impervious *to* argument
Implicated *in* a crime
Incidental *to* a thing
Inclined *to* sloth
Incumbent *on* a person
Indebted *to* a person
Indebtedness *for* beneficence bestowed
Indebted *in* a large sum of money
Independent *of* someone, something
Indifferent *to* heat and cold
Indigenous *to* a country
Indignant *at* insults heaped
Indignant *with* a person
Indispensable *to* success
Indulgent *to* children
Indulgent *in* wine
Infatuated *with* someone

Infected *with* disease
Infested *with* ants
Inflicted *on* a person
Informed *of* an incident
Inimical *to* a person
Innocent *of* a charge
Insensitive *to* something
Insensible *to* shame
Inspired *with* confidence
Intent *on* doing a thing
Interested *in* a person or thing
Intimate *with* a person
Introduced *into* an office
Introduced *to* a person
Inured *to* drudgery
Invested *with* powers
Invested *in* RBI bonds
Involved *in* criminal activities
Irrelevant *to* the query made
Irrespective *of* consequences
Jarring *to* ears
Jealous *of* her success
Lame *of* a leg
Lavish *in* expending
Lavish *of* money
Lax *in* character
Level *with* the floor
Liable *to* make mistakes
Liable *for* payment
Liberal *in* approach
Liberal *for* advice
Limited *to* a purpose
Loyal *to* the establishment
Mad *with* joy
Made *for* each other
Made *of* wood

Meddlesome *in* others' works
Material *to* success
Mindful *of* the promises made
Mistaken *for* someone else
Mistrustful *of* someone
Moved *to* tears
Moved *with* pity
Moved *at* the sight
Moved *by* entreaties
Natural *to* a person
Necessity *to* life
Negligent *in* work
Negligent *of* duty
Notorious *for* misdeeds
Obedient *to* elders
Obligatory *on* your part
Obliged *to* someone
Obliged *for* help received
Oblivious *of* the dangers ahead
Obnoxious *to* someone
Observant *of* facts
Obstinate *in* resistance
Obstructive *to* a project
Occupied *with* some work
Occupied *in* reading documents
Odious *to* a person
Offended *at* something
Offended *with* someone
Offensive *to* someone
Officious *in* conduct
Ominous *of* disasters
Open *to* flattery
Opposed *to* realities
Overcome *with* grief
Overwhelmed *with* grief
Painful *to* feelings

Parallel *to* anything
Parallel *with* anything
Paramount *to* anything
Partial *to* someone
Peculiar *to* a thing or person
Penance *for* sin
Penitence *for* past misdeeds
Penurious *in* habits
Pertinent *to* a question
Polite *in* manners
Polite *to* strangers
Poor *in* attitude
Popular *for* his tricks
Popular *with* friends
Possessed *of* wealth
Possessed *with* an idea
Precious *to* an office
Precluded *from* doing a thing
Prefixed *to* a document
Prejudicial *to* one's interests
Preliminary *to* an inquiry
Preparatory *to* a probe
Prepared *for* the worst
Productive *of* wealth
Proficient *in* English
Profuse *in* praises
Prone *to* falling ill
Proper *for* the occasion
Proud *of* his treasure
Purged *of* evil thoughts
Pursuant *to* an inquiry
Qualified *for* the job
Quarrelsome *by* nature
Quarrelsome *with* everyone
Quick *of* understanding
Quick *at* resolving problems

Radiant *with* smile
Ready *for* action
Ready *at* accounts
Ready *in* or *with* answers
Receptive *of* ideas
Reckless *of* expenses
Reconciled *to* a situation
Reconciled *with* adversaries
Redolent *of* smoke
Reduced *to* poverty
Regardless *of* consequences
Related *to* a person
Relative *to* a question
Relevant *to* the point
Remiss *in* duties
Repentant *of* his sins
Replete *with* things of joy
Repugnant *to* established laws of the land
Repulsive *to* ideas
Requisite *to* happiness
Requisite *for* a purpose
Resolved *on* doing a thing
Respectful *to* or towards seniors
Responsible *for* one's actions
Responsible *to* an office or person
Restricted *to* a particular thing
Reticent *about* speaking, *in* manner
Revenge *on* a person
Rich *in* something
Rid *of* troubles
Sacred *to* memory
Sanguine *of* victory
Satiated *with* pleasures of life
Satisfied *with* results
Scornful *of* a person
Secure *from* harm

Secure *against* attack
Sensitive *to* criticism
Shocked *at* behaviour
Shocking *to* sensibilities
Short *of* fund
Sick *of* excuses
Silent *about* something
Similar *to* a thing or person
Simultaneous *with* an incident
Skilful *in* doing a thing
Skilful *at* an activity
Skilful *with* tools
Slothful *in* action
Slow *at* reacting
Slow *of* hearing
Slow *in* deciding
Solicitous *of* an answer
Solicitous *for* someone's safety and security
Sorry *for* the inconvenience caused
Spiteful *against* a person
Startled *at* a sight
Steeped *in* vice
Strange *to* a person
Subject *to* approval
Subordinate *to* a person
Subsequent *to* some incident
Subsidiary *to* business
Subsist *on* allowances
Subversive *of* authority
Sufficient *for* a purpose
Suitable *for* life
Suitable *to* the occasion
Suited *for* the post
Suited *to* the occasion
Sure *of* success
Suspicious *of* intents

Sympathetic *with* the injured
Synonymous *with* another expression
Tantamount *to* perjury
Temperate *in* habits
Tenacious *of* purpose
Thankful *for* helps extended
Tired *of* idleness
Tired *with* his forays into forests
True *to* his beliefs
Uneasy *about* the fallout
Used *to* (accustomed)
Used *for* (applied)
Useful *for* a purpose
Vain *of* his achievements
Veiled *in* mystery
Versed *in* Shakespearean
Vested *in* a person
Vexed *at* a thing
Vexed *with* a person
Vexed *about, at* something
Victorious *over* miseries
Void *of* substance

Verbs followed by prepositions:-
Abide *by* rules, agreement
Abide *with* someone
Abide *in* him or her (transitive)
Abound *in* or *with* fish
Absolve *of* or *from* a charge
Abstain *from* vice
Abut *on, against* land
Accede *to* a request
Accord *in* or *with* (an opinion)
Accord *to* a person
Account *for* a thing or person
Account *to* a person

Accrue *to* a person
Accuse *of* some mischief
Acquiesce *in* a decision, *to* pressure
Acquit *of* blame or charge
Adapt *to* situations
Adept *at* an activity
Adept *in* an art
Adhere *to* a plan
Admit *to, into* ('let in')
Admit *of* an excuse
Admit *into* or *to* a secret
Advert *on* something
Agree *to, on, upon* a proposal or terms
Agree *about* (concur)
Argue *with* a person
Argue *over, about* a situation or thing
Argue *for* or *against* a position
Agree *with* a person, *in* a specified manner
Aim *at* a target
Alight *from* aircraft
Alight *on* the ground
Allot *to* a person
Allow *of* delay
Allude *to* an incident
Alternate *with* something else
Anchor *off* the shore
Animadvert *on* one's shortcomings
Answer *for* conduct
Answer *to* a call
Apologise *to* a person
Apologise *for* misconduct
Appeal *to* an authority
Appeal *for* redress of grievances
Appeal *against* an order
Apply *to* an authority *for* a thing
Apprise *of* a fact

Approve *of* a plan of actions
Arbitrate *between* two warring groups
Arrive *at* a place
Arrive *in* a country
Ascribe *to* a cause
Ask *for* a thing
Ask *of* or *from* a person
Aspire *after* wealth
Aspire *to* some particular thing
Assent *to* agreed terms
Associate *with* a person or thing
Assure *of* a fact to a person
Atone *for* some sinful acts committed
Attain *to* a height
Attend *to* something or to a speaker
Attend *on* a person
Attribute *to* a cause
Avail *of* certain facilities
Avenge *on* a person
Avert *from* a person
Badger *into* doing something
Badger *about* a situation
Ban *from* a place
Bank *on* (rely) something, someone (not *upon*)
Bank *at*, *with* a financial institution
Bark *at* a person or thing
Bask *in* glory
Based *on* (not *upon*) a premise
Based *in* a place, a field of study
Bear *with* one's impatience
Beat *against* the rocks
Beat *on* one's head
Become *of* someone (what will become of you?)
Beg pardon *of* a person
Beg a person *to* do a thing
Beg *for* something from someone

Begin *with* the first named
Beguile *into* doing something
Beguiled *with* gifts, flattery
Believe *in* one's honour
Belong *to* a person
Bequeath a thing *to* posterity
Bestow a thing *on* a person
Beware *of* pickpockets
Blame a person *for* something
Blush *at* one's foolishness
Blush *for* others' foolishness
Boast or brag *of* one's achievements
Borrow *of* or *from* a person
Break *into* a house (burglary)
Break *through* restraint
Break oneself *of* a habit
Break ill news *to* someone
Break *with* a person
Bring a thing *to* light
Bring a thing *under* notice
Brood *over* past failures
Burst *into* a rage
Burst *upon* a country
Buy a thing *of* a person
Buy a thing *from* a shop
Cajole *into* doing something
Cajole *out* of a possession
Caution *against* doing something
Call *on* a person
Call *for* retribution
Call *to* a person
Canvass *for* support
Care *for* children
Carp *at* someone's conduct
Catch *at* an opportunity
Cavil *at* an action

Cease *from* doing a thing
Censure *for* a fault
Challenge *to* duel
Chafe *at* doing something
Chafe *under* an irritating authority
Charge *with* crime
Charge payment *to* a person
Cheat someone *of* his dues
Clamour *for* better wages
Clear a person *of* blame
Cling *to* a point or person
Coalesce *with* something else
Coalesce *into* a unit
Coerce *into* doing something
Coincide *with* something
Collude *with* a person to defraud another
Commiserate *with* a person
Combat *with* hardships
Come *across* a friend (accidental meeting)
Come *into* vogue
Come *by* thing (obtainment of a thing)
Come *of* something (result from)
Come *to* fifty five (amount to)
Commence *with* a thing
Communicate *to* a person
Communicate *with* a person on a specific matter
Compare *with* a person
Compare *to* a thing
Comply *with* rule, an order
Compensate *for* a loss suffered
Compete *with* one another *for* a prize
Complain *of* something to a person
Complain *against* a person
Conceal details *from* a person
Concede *to* demands
Concur *with* a person

Concur *in* an opinion
Condemn *to* death
Condemn *for* murder committed
Condole *with* a person
Conduce *to* joy
Confer a title *on* someone (this is transitive verb)
Confer *with* a person on a given topic (this is intransitive verb)
Confess *to* a mistake made
Confide information *to* someone (this is transitive use of verb)
Confide *in* someone's honour (this is intransitive use of verb)
Conform *to* rules and views of another person
Congratulate *on* success
Connive *at* others' faults
Connive *with* someone in doing a thing
Consent *to* something
Consign *to* dustbin
Consists *in* something (data related matter or facts)
Consists *of* something (material)
Consult *with* a person
Content *with* or *against* a person
Content *for* or *above* a thing
Contribute *to* something
Converge *on* something
Converge *to* a point
Converse *with* someone *about* a thing
Convict someone *of* a crime
Convince someone *of* a fact
Cope *with* a problem
Correspond *with* someone (write a letter)
Correspond *to* something (agree on a point)
Count *on* a thing
Count *for* nothing
Crave *for* or *after* pleasures of life
Credit *with* good intents or money
Crow *over* a lost cause
Cure *of* a disease

Cut *in* or *to* pieces
Dabble *in* astronomy
Dally *with* someone
Dash *against* a thing
Dash *over* a thing
Dash *for* a destination
Dawn *on* a person
Deal *well* or ill by a person
Deal *in* spices
Deal *with* a person or *with* a subject
Debar *from* doing a thing
Debit *with* a sum of amount
Decide *on* something
Decide *against* something
Declare *for* something
Declare *against* something
Defend *someone* against harm
Defer *to* someone's wishes
Defraud a person *of* his hard earned money
Deliberate *on* a matter
Deliver *from* a difficulty
Deluge *with* fund
Demand something *of* a person
Demur *to* a statement
Depend *on* someone
Deprive *of* something
Derogate *from* someone's reputation
Descant *on* a subject
Desist *from* an attempt
Despair *of* riches
Despoil a child *of* his toys and dolls
Deter a person *from* doing a thing
Determine *on* what to do
Detract *from* the facts
Deviate *from* the main issue
Devolves *on* a person to do his acclaimed duty

Die *of* diarrhoea
Die *from* overwork or *from* violence
Differ *with* a person *on* a matter
Differ *from* a thing or quality
Differ *about, over, on* an issue
Digress *from* the point of discussion
Dilate *on* a given subject matter
Dip *into* a subject
Disable *from* doing a thing
Disagree *with* a person
Disapprove *of* a thing
Dispense *with* services
Dispose *of* property
Dispute *with* a person about a thing or two
Disseize *of* an estate (dispossess)
Dissent *from, against* an opinion
Dissimilar *to* (not *from*)
Dissociate *from* something, someone
Distinguish one *from* another
Distinguish *between* two things
Divert one's attention *from* something
Divest *of* something
Divide *in* half
Divide *into* six pieces
Dote *on* a thing or person
Domineer *over* an inferior
Dream *of* bizarre things
Drive *at* a point
Drop *out* of the school
Drop *off* a tree
Dwell *on* a topic
Eat *into* something
Elicit *from* a person
Embark *on* board a ship
Embark *in* business
Emerge *from* the crowd

Employ *in* a job
Encroach *on* one's fiefdom
Endorse *with* a signature and delivery
Endow *with* largesse
Enjoin *on* a person
Enlarge *on* bail
Enlarge *on* a subject
Enlist *in* the army
Enlist someone *in* some project
Ensconced *in* an ivory tower
Enter *upon* a career
Enter *into* a tunnel
Entitle someone *to* an estate
Entrust someone *with* a job
Entrust a thing *to* someone
Err *on the* side of leniency
Escape *from* night long drudgery
Exact a promise *from* someone
Excel *in* something
Excerpt *from* something(n & v)
Exchange one thing *for* another
Exchange *with* a person
Exclude *from* a responsibility
Excuse a person *from* attending to a function
Exempt a person *from* doing a thing
Exonerate a person *from* blame
Expiate *on* a matter
Explain *to* someone
Expostulate *with* a person
Exult *in* victory *over* an adversary
Fail *in* an attempt
Fall *amongst* thieves
Fall *in* love
Fall *in* with one's opinions
Fall *on* the enemy
Fall *into* a trap

Fall *under* someone's displeasure
Fawn *on* a person
Feed *on* victuals (intransitive use of verb)
Feed a cow *with* fodder (verb transitively used)
Feel *for* a person in distress
Fight *for* the weak *against* the strong
Fight *with* or *against* a person
Flirt *with* a person
Fly *at* a dog
Fly *into* rage
Foreclose *on* mortgaged property
Fraternize *with* certain people
Free *of* or *from* anything
Furnish *with* a thing
Furnish *to* a person
Gain *on* someone in a race
Get *at* the facts
Get *over* a trauma
Get *on* with a person
Get *out* of bad habits
Get *to* the tether post
Glance *at* an object
Glance *over* a document
Glory *in* success
Grapple *with* difficulties
Grasp *at* something
Grieve *for* a person lost
Grieve *at* or *for* or *about* an incident
Grumble *at* one's lot
Guard *against* a lurking danger
Guess *at* something
Hail *as* (an esteemed person)
Hail *from* a place
Hanker *after* money
Happen *to* a person
Heal *of* a disease

Hear *of* an event
Hesitate *at* nothing
Hinder one *from* doing something
Hide something *from* someone
Hinge *on* something
Hint *at* an event likely to occur
Hope *for* freedom
Hover *over* the head
Hunt *after* or *for* something
Impart *to* a person
Import *into* a country
Import *from* a country
Impose *on* (not *upon*) a person
Impress *on* a person (an idea)
Impress *with* an idea (a person)
Impute *to* a person (blame)
Incite *to* action, *to* rebellion
Increase *in* wisdom
Inculcate *on* a person
Inculcate *into*, *in* a person
Indict a person *for* some crime committed
Indorse *with* a signature
Indulge *in* vulgarity
Indulge *with* wine and other vices
Infer *from* something
Inflict *on* a man
Inform *of* a thing
Inform *against* a man
Infringe *on* others' rights
Initiate someone *into* an order
Inquire *into* a matter
Inquire *of* a person *about* or *concerning* some matter
Inquire *after* people
Insist *on* something
Inspire *with* courage
Instil *in*, *into* a person

Intercede *with* someone for someone else
Interfere *with* someone *in* some matter
Intersect *with* each other
Introduce a man *to* someone
Introduce *into* a place
Intrude *on* one's privacy
Intrude *into* one's house
Intrust a person *with* a thing
Intrust a thing *to* a person
Inveigh *against* wrong done
Inveigle *into* a trap
Invest *in* some scheme
Invest *with* authority
Invite *to* dinner
Involve *in* debt
Issue *from* some source
Jeer *at* a person
Jest *at* a person
Join *in* a business
Join a thing *into* another
Judge *of* something
Jump *at* an offer
Jump *to* a conclusion
Keep *to* the point
Keep *from* alcohol
Kick *against* someone
Kick *at* a thing
Knock head *against* a wall
Knock *at* the door
Know *of* a person
Lament *for* the dead
Languish *for* comfort
Lapse *into* idleness
Laugh *at* a person
Laugh *to* deride
Lay facts *before* an authority

Lay a person *under* obligation
Lean *against* a wall
Lean *on* a baton
Lean *to* a certain viewpoint
Level *with* ground
Lie *in* one's power
Lie *under* an imputation
Listen *to* complaints
Listen *for* a dissenting note
Live *by* honest labour
Live *for* riches or fame
Live *on* a meagre allowance
Live *within* one's means
Long *for* or *after* something
Look *after* something
Look *at* a thing or person
Look *into* a matter
Look *for* something
Look *over* an account
Look *through* an account
Look *out* of a place
Lull *into* silence (deception)
Lull *to* sleep
Lust *after* riches
Make *away* with goods
Make *for* happiness
Make *up* to an adversary
Make some sense *of* a nuisance
Marry a person *to* another
Marvel *at* some sight or incident
Match *with* something
Meant *as* an intention
Meant *for* a destination
Meddle *in* someone's domain
Meddle *with* others' business
Mediate *with* someone

Meditate *on* something
Meet *with* a rebuff
Merge *into* anything
Merge *with* something
Militate *against* an outcome
Mortgage *to* someone
Mourn *for* the dead
Muse *upon* something
Object *to* some remarks
Occur *to* one's mind
Offend *against* civil behaviour
Officiate *for* someone
Operation *on* a patient
Originate *in* a thing or place
Originate *with* a person
Overwhelm *with* benedictions
Pall *on* something
Pall *of* darkness
Part *with* a thing or person
Partake *of* some food
Participate *with* a person in his profit
Pass *for* an intelligent person
Pass *from* one thing *into* another
Pass *by* a train
Pass *over* something
Pay *for* one's folly
Perish *by* the sword
Perish *with* cold
Persevere *with* an effort
Persist *in* doing a thing
Pertain or pertaining *to* a question
Pine *for* food
Plead *with* someone *for* relief
Plot *against* a man
Plunge *into* an abyss
Ponder *over* or *on* a subject

Pounce *on* something
Pray *for* forgiveness
Prefer this *to* that
Prepare *for* the worst
Prepare *against* disaster
Present *with* something
Pretend *to* omniscience
Prevail *on* a person
Prevail *against* or *over* an enemy
Prevail *with* a person
Prevent *from* parting
Prey *upon* something
Pride oneself *on* an achievement
Proceed *with* a business
Proceed *to* a business
Proceed *from* one end *to* another
Proceed *against* the erring employee
Prohibit *from* smoking
Protect *from* injury
Protest *against* ill-treatment
Provide *for* one's family
Provide *against* the rainy days
Provide *with* something
Provoke *to* anger
Pry *into* privacy
Punish *for* a fault
Purge the mind *of* evil thoughts
Purge *from* an organization, a society
Quake *with* fear
Qualify *for* a post
Quarrel *with* someone *over* or *about* something
Quote *from* something
Rail *at* or *against* someone
Reason *with* a person *on* or *about* a thing
Rebel *against* the state
Reckon *on* something

Reckon *with* a person
Recoil *from* a sight
Reconcile *to* a loss
Reconcile *with* an adversary
Recover *from* an ailment
Refer *to* a subject
Refrain *from* doing a thing
Rejoice *at* the success
Rejoice *in* one's own success
Relapse *into* coma
Relieve *of* or *from* pain
Rely *on* someone
Remind *of* a thing
Remonstrate *with* a person *against* something said or done
Repose confidence *in* someone
Reprimand *for* a lapse
Resolve *on* a course of action
Rest *on* laurels, *on* couch, *on* facts
Rest *with* a person
Retaliate *on* an enemy
Retract *from* a given statement
Revel *in* vice
Revenge *on* someone *for* injury caused
Revert *to* something
Revolt *against* the system
Reward *with* something *for* a job done
Rob *of* something
Rule *over* a country
Run *after* money
Run *at* something
Run *into* bad weather
Run *over* an account
Run *through* one's savings
Save *from* injury or harm
Scoff *at* traditions
Search *for* something

Search *into* a matter
See *to* a matter
See *through* one's designs
See *about* a matter
See *into* a matter
Seek *for* or *after* peace
Send *for* a carpenter
Sentence someone *to* a fine
Set *about* a task
Set *on* course
Set *upon* something
Set *up* a business
Shiver *at* something
Shiver *from* cold or some thought
Shudder *at* the very thought
Side *with* a person in distress
Sit *over* a matter
Sit *under* an imputation
Smell *of* foul odour
Smile *at* one's remarks
Smile *on* a person
Snap *at* a person
Snatch *at* a straw
Speak *of* a subject
Speak *on* a subject
Speculate *in* shares
Speculate *on* the future course of action
Stand *against* an enemy
Stand *by* a friend in need
Stand *on* one's dignity
Stand *on* one's views
Stare *at* a person
Stare a person *in* the face
Start *for* Patna
Stick *to* a point
Stick *at* nothing

Stigmatize *as* dishonourable
Stoop *to* conquer
Strike *at* something
Strike *on* a boulder
Strike *for* better emoluments
Strip *of* title
Struggle *against* odds
Subject one to ridicule
Submit *to* authority
Subscribe *to* a periodical or an opinion
Subscribe *for* a stock
Subsist *on* bare minimum
Succeed *to* an estate
Succeed *in* an endeavour
Succeed *as* a person in some position
Succumb *to* injuries
Sue *for* defamation
Surrender *to* the enemy
Sympathise *with* a person
Take *after* her mother (refers to resemblance)
Take a person *for* a thief
Take *to* drinking
Take *upon* oneself to do a thing
Talk *of* or *about* an incident
Talk *over* an issue
Talk *with* or *to* a person
Tamper *with* documents
Taste *of* milk
Tell *about* or *of* an event
Testify *to* a fact
Think *of* or *about* a thing
Think *over* a matter
Threaten *with* dire consequences
Throw something *at* someone
Tide *over* difficulties
Touch *at* the harbour

Touch *upon* a subject
Tower *over* others
Trade for swap
Trade *in* (sell)
Trade *with* (do business with)
Trade *at* (patronize)
Trade *on* (buy and sell)
Trespass *against* rules
Trespass *on* someone's time or privacy
Trespass *in* someone's house
Trifle *with* someone's sentiments
Triumph *over* difficulties
Trust *in* a person
Trust *to* a man's integrity
Trust someone *with* something valuable
Turn steel *into* gold
Turn *to* someone *for* help
Upbraid someone *with* ingratitude
Urge *upon* authorities to do/deliver justice
Urge a matter *on* someone's notice
Venture *upon* a journey
Vie *for* honour *with* another person
Vote *for* solidarity
Vote *against* tyranny
Wait *at* the sight
Wait *for* someone or something
Warn *of* danger
Warn *against* a fault
Wink *at* one's deficiencies
Wish *for* something
Work *for* small allowance
Work *at* aeronautics
Wrestle *with* an adversary
Wriggle *out* of trouble
Writhe *with* pain
Yearn *for* attention

Yield *to* popular demand

Adjectives followed by Prepositions:

Adverbs are followed by the same **prepositions/adjectives** as shown in the table given below:

Prepositions preceded by adverbs	Prepositions preceded by adjectives
Adversely *to* one's interests	Adverse *to* one's interest
Agreeably *to* one's expectations	Agreeable *to* one's expectations
Angrily *with* a friend	Angry *with* a friend
Anxiously *for* one's escape	Anxious *for* one's escape
Appropriately *to* the occasion	Appropriate *to* the occasion
Conditionally *on* something happening	Conditional *on* something happening
Compatibly *with* logic	Compatible *with* logic
Comfortably *with* logic	Comfortable *with* logic
Conformably *to* logic	Conformable *to* logic
Consistently *with* logic	Consistent *with* logic
Effectively *for* an intent	Effective *for* an intent
Favourably *to* one's interest	Favourable *to* one's interest
Fortunately *for* one	Fortunate *for* one
Independently *of* something	Independent *of* something
Irrelevantly *to* a question	Irrelevant *to* a question
Irreverently *of* a thing	Irreverent *of* a thing
Irrespectively *of* consequences	Irrespective *of* consequences
Loyalty *to* the government	Loyal *to* the government
Obstructively *to* freedom	Obstructive *to* freedom
Offensively *to* superiors	Offensive *to* superiors
Prejudicially *to* one's interests	Prejudicial *to* one's interests
Previously *to* some event	Previous *to* some event
Profitably *to* one's own self	Profitable *to* one's own self
Proportionately *to* something	Proportionate *to* something
Simultaneously *with* an event	Simultaneous *with* an event
Subsequently *to* some event	Subsequent *to* some event
Sufficiently *for* the task	Sufficient *for* the task

□

Usage

There are, generally, four levels of usage in English. They are:

♦ **Formal Language**–It is used in government, legal, scholarly, and other similar 'official' contexts; it often uses technical terms and stylized forms of expressions.

♦ **Standard Language**–It is a written language that is characteristic of educated people and is usually called 'semi-official' or 'edited' English.

♦ **Informal or Familiar Language**–This is used in more relaxed, usually unconversational contexts. This level of language covers a broad range of usage that includes everything from coined words and phrases to jargon, dialect, slang and shoptalk.

♦ **Substandard Language**–This means language that is generally deemed unacceptable by the literate community, but is nevertheless commonly understood. It can also include archaism or obsolete language.

Wordiness, jargon, cliché and euphemisms are marks of poor usage and are usually avoided in quality writings.

□

Spoken English

English used in our day-to-day conversations is what we call spoken English. Written language always follows a definite rule of grammar, but conversational language often takes liberties, not necessarily grammatical liberties, not frowned upon. This is because the language we speak is usually informal and therefore digressive to some extent. Written language on the other hand is formal in nature and needs to conform to the requirements of grammatical rules. We have discussed some of those key rules in the foregoing pages. We now turn to conversational English. In conversational English even though there are no set rules, grammatical rules are generally followed with occasional digressions. This helps to keep the conversation lively and interesting and at the same time intelligible enough for the listeners. Given below are some typical conversations that may come handy for those who are keen to start speaking in English:

1) Conversation between two friends who meet after many years.

Venkat: Hey, you! Aren't you Paresh?
Paresh: Oh, Venkat! What a pleasant surprise!
Venkat: Very pleasant surprise indeed to see an old friend at such a new place!
Paresh: How come you here?
Venkat: I have come to join my duty...but how about you? How come you here?
Paresh: This is my place of domicile and also my place of work.

You said you have come to join duty here...which dept. are you going to join?

Venkat: I am here to report to LHO of State Bank. I am sure you can guide me to the office.

Paresh: Guide you? I'll take you there. It's not very far away from where my residence is.

Venkat: But there is time for that. Take me to a hotel in the meantime so that I can have a shower and good brunch before I proceed to the bank.

Paresh: You are my guest here...don't you talk about hotel and things like that...didn't I tell you my residence is not very far away from your bank?

Venkat: Yes, you did indeed. But I would not like to bother you...in any case bank is going to foot the bill for my lodging and boarding.

Paresh: I couldn't care any less for what your bank is going to do for you. You are my guest here for now.

Venkat: Look, Paresh! I'll be here for two months.

Paresh: All right! You may shift to the accommodation provided by the bank, but for now let's go to my place and do not argue.

Venkat: Well, you have always been like this...having your own way.

Paresh: Come on, friend...we have met after these many years... how can I deprive myself the joy of your company, even if a brief one? Besides, won't you like to meet your Bhabhi?

Venkat: With pleasure...so you have married, is it?

Paresh: Just this year...had I known about you, I would have had the pleasure of having you in the marriage. Most of our old friends were there. Nair is also here.

Venkat: Oh great! That means I have not landed in an alien land.

Paresh: Of course, not...and how about your marriage?

Venkat: Well, my parents are pressing me hard...I have requested them to wait for my training to end. Six months to go for my probation to end.

Paresh: What is this training?

Venkat: I am a probationary officer and I have come to this place for an on-the-job training for two months...in this way we are exposed to various aspects of banking for two years before being put into line banking.

Paresh: All right...let's go now. There will be time to talk about all this later.

Venkat: Yeah, let's go.

2) Conversation between father and son

Father: So, son! What's happening?

Son: Readying for the battle ahead.

Father: What kind of battle, son?

Son: Getting a good job is nothing short of a battle these days.

Father: Absolutely right...and how are you preparing for that battle?

Son: A little undecided at the moment...in about two months' time there will be a campus selection in our college. We are all keyed up on that. We are all gearing ourselves up to meet the expectations of our prospective employers.

Father: What precisely are you doing to impress them?

Son: Nothing specific. But as you have always advised, I am trying to keep to the basics.

Father: And how exactly are you doing that?

Son: By trying to master my subject.

Father: Yes, that is very important. Knowing your subject well gives you the confidence. Without confidence, you cannot impress your buyers. In today's world every individual is on sale...we have all been reduced to being a commodity in today's globalised market. A buyer looks for the best commodity. An individual having knowledge and ability to adjust to new demands and challenges is the commodity the modern buyers look for.

Son: I remember these words of yours and I am preparing myself accordingly.

Father: You are on the right track, my son. I am sure you will achieve the objective. Your endeavour should be to try to excel. God bless you!

Son: I'll like you to hold a mock interview for me. Who could be a better interviewer than you?

Father: All right then. Get ready for a showdown tomorrow evening. Expect no leniency from me and come duly prepared; and be formally dressed for the occasion.

Son: Okay; and thank you, Papa.

3) Conversation between a senior level and a junior level official

Senior: What happened to the project I had asked you to repare?

Junior: I am on the job, sir.

Senior: How long does it take to complete such a small project? It's already been a week since I assigned you the task. What's delaying it?

Junior: Actually, sir, I am expecting some data from the Block Office.

Senior: Three days ago also you cited the same reason...what's the problem in getting the data?

Junior: BDO informed me that the head clerk has gone on leave for marriage of his daughter. He has not returned yet...and the relevant file is in his almirah.

Senior: That means until he returns, nothing can be done?

Junior: Sir, I am trying to get the job done at the earliest.

Senior: Well, I can see that. Presently you speak to BDO and ask him to furnish the data immediately, head clerk or no head clerk. What kind of information it is that BDO does not have? What period does it relate to?

Junior: It relates to the last financial year.

Senior: You do not have the data of the last financial year...what kind of a job are you doing?

Junior: Sir, because of strike by the NGEs, data compilation has suffered.

Senior: But the project report is about the previous financial year...why do you need the data of the last financial year? Well, you are not serious about the task that is assigned to you and I certainly don't like this kind of apathetical attitude. Complete the project immediately...and I want no excuses such as these.

Junior: Sir.

4) Conversation between husband and wife

Wife: Shiela tells me there is an art exhibition at Gandhi Maidan. Why don't you take leave for a day tomorrow so that we could spend some quality time there?

Husband: News spreads faster by word of mouth even in this age of fast communication, is it?

Wife: Should that be a problem?

Husband: None at all...only I was wondering Shiela of all the persons should inform you about art exhibition.

Wife: Why, what's wrong in that? Do you mean Shiela has no sense of art?

Husband: Oh, no. Do I dare?

Wife: You had better not. So, you are taking leave tomorrow?

Husband: Leave? What for?

Wife: Well, for art exhibition at Gandhi Maidan; to spend some quality time.

Husband: Aren't we spending enough of a quality time together here that we should go to Gandhi Maidan?

Wife: Now stop this insinuating talk of yours and tell me whether you are taking leave tomorrow?

Husband: My boss will shoot me dead if I spoke about leave...why don't you reserve it for some other occasion?

Wife: For the past two decades I have been trying to get to that occasion.

Husband: Now that's being unfair.

Wife: Unfair! Can you recall an occasion when we went out for any such thing?

Husband: Last week we saw a movie together, didn't we?

Wife: Great achievement indeed. What else?

Husband: All right, we will go to see that art exhibition this Sunday. No excuses at all. I promise. And we will dine out.

Wife: But why Sunday? You can't have quality time on Sundays.

Husband: My dear, Sunday is the only day when I am free. Please see reason.

Wife: All right...then it is fixed. Sunday–art exhibition.

Husband: Yeah, Sunday.

5) Two students discussing their prospects for getting admission to IITs

Rohan: Hi, Abhi! What are you doing?

Abhi: Preparing for IIT, what else?

Rohan: Yeah, but where are you going for coaching?

Abhi: Papa says, I should prepare here itself. But I want to go to Kota...and what are you doing?

Rohan: I am going to Delhi, to my uncle...he says there are good institutions in Delhi.

Abhi: Well, you have your uncle...I have very limited choice.

Rohan: Why! You too can come...we can prepare together. I am sure my uncle will have no problem. He has a massive house with attendants.

Abhi: Papa will not agree.

Rohan: I'll also request uncle to let you go with me.

Abhi: He has a problem with Delhi.

Rohan: Problem with Delhi? Why?

Abhi: He says Delhi will have far too many distractions not good for students. Kota has none. At Kota all you get to do is to study...there is nothing there except studies. You don't get to go anywhere, no movies, no distractions at all...studying is a full-time occupation there.

Rohan: But we do not want to become book worms...don't you think some entertainment is necessary both for body and mind?

Abhi: Is it material what I think? Besides, the need of competing for IIT puts everything else to a secondary position.

Rohan: Of course, the competition is very tough and this leaves very little scope for other things. But we need to give some recreation to ourselves.

Abhi: True, but the immediate need is to get into IIT. I dread the idea of failing to make it. What shall I do if I don't make it?

Rohan: IIT is not the end of the road...there are many other institutions. Don't think so seriously on that.

Abhi: Papa is very keen that I get into IIT...he says he had not got the opportunity. I must make-up for that.

Rohan: This is not fair. You must not put extra burden on yourself. Together we can discuss the matter with your papa and make him flexible.

Abhi: Yeah, we can. But I am not sure if we will be able to ready him for anything short of IIT.

Rohan: Let's try to convince him first. Then we'll see what can be done.

Abhi: Yeah, let's try. But I am worried all the same.

6) Conversation between a boy and a girl

Mona: You made me wait so long. What were you doing?

Ravi: I am sorry, Mona. It was the traffic.

Mona: Was it traffic or something else?

Ravi: Well, you must trust me. There was a big jam at the main road.

Mona: I did not see any jam anywhere.

Ravi: That is because you came from the other end of the road...it's free on that side. The problem is on this side of the main road....

Mona: All right...what happened to that job you had applied for?

Ravi: I have sent my CV. Hope to get call soon.

Mona: What, haven't you got the call as yet? Nili too had applied to the same company. She has been called for interview tomorrow.

Ravi: I haven't checked my mail today. May be, they have sent something for me as well.

Mona: Why don't you check it here? Let's go to that cyber café.

Ravi: I have taken a look there...it's crowded. When did you get to know about Nili?

Mona: She informed me in the morning as I was readying for my office. I wished her all the best. In fact, she asked me if you were also going for interview tomorrow. I thought she was keen to go with you.

Ravi: All right, let's move in to the cyber café and wait for my turn.

Mona: Let's first go to a restaurant...I want steaming hot coffee. I have waited long enough in this shivering cold.

Ravi: Okay, let's go and enjoy coffee.

Mona: I find Nili has been taking more interest in you these days...anything the matter?

Ravi: It would be foolish of her to take any interest in me.

Mona: Why?

Ravi: Well, she knows me well enough to know my area of interest.

Mona: Area of interest can change, can't it?

Ravi: Not mine. I am not so sure about yours....

Mona: Is it loss of confidence or something else?

Ravi: Both.

Mona: Why should you think that?

Ravi: You have a job. I have none. This will explain loss of confidence.

Mona: And something else?

Ravi: Loss of confidence could lead to anything.

Mona: Have no fears...I am sure you are going to get the call...and not just the call, you are going to get the job.

Ravi: Thanks for boosting my morale.

Mona: Did you need this boosting?

Ravi: Yes, particularly after you said Nili was taking interest in me.

Mona: Oh, that was just a joke, to tease you out of your laziness.

Ravi: Nice to hear that...otherwise, you know, things change very fast these days...nothing seems permanent here now.

Mona: True, but the situation is not that hopeless.

Ravi: Of course, not.

7) Conversation between two senior citizens

Kumar Saheb: Halo, Singh Saheb, how is everything? Seeing you after a long time.

Singh Saheb: Yes, it's been long time indeed. I had been to Mumbai. But what a difficult question you asked.

Kumar Saheb: Difficult question?

Singh Saheb: Difficult question indeed. Who can answer how is everything? Is it not a difficult question?

Kumar Saheb: Yes, if you take it literally.

Singh Saheb: No choice, but to take literally...and though the question is difficult, it is our duty to find some answer to it.

Kumar Saheb: Yes, of course, it is important to look back and see how far we have travelled and whether we have taken the right path.

Singh Saheb: 60 years have gone by since we have attained independence and in these years our population has increased manifold. We have made long strides and achieved many things.

Kumar Saheb: The quality of life has also improved.

Singh Saheb: Yes, mechanization has improved the quality of our life...but the moot point is—have they really improved it?

Kumar Saheb: Why, don't you think there has been a qualitative change in our life?

Singh Saheb: Yes, a qualitative change for the worse....earlier we were all living together. Now you hardly find anybody with you.

Kumar Saheb: That is a thing of the past. We no longer have joint families. But we cannot complain because we wanted it.

Singh Saheb: I did not want it. So, I can complain. Look at the shape and the size of the world. The population of the world has increased manifold; we have become progressively lonely. We are all alone. None of our children is with us. They are all out to earn money.

Kumar Saheb: Yes, and that is an important thing to do. We cannot have them with us in our homes. The whole world is now one global market. Jobs are spread out to the whole world and if one wishes to compete, one has to go out and earn livelihood.

Singh Saheb: Is earning livelihood the only objective of life? Does it make us happy? Are we enjoying our life?

Kumar Saheb: That's a difficult question to answer. Some compromises have to be made. The need of earning money cannot be overlooked.

Singh Saheb: We too earned money. Money has always been important. But today it has become all-important. Money is the new god and this god has replaced all other gods. This is what makes life so ugly. Look around you, you'll hardly find a thing that gives you comfort...hardly anything to instil confidence. It makes me sad to see the kind of world we are bequeathing to our children.

Kumar Saheb: Well, things aren't really that bad as they appear to you.

Singh Saheb: I should be happy to be proved wrong.

8) A child is kidnapped; and ransom is demanded from the parent. What follows is a conversation between the kidnapper and the victim's parent

Kidnapper: Halo, is it Shyamlal?

Parent: Yes, Shyamlal here, who is calling?

Kidnapper: Never mind that...now listen carefully to what I have to say....

Parent: Yes!

Kidnapper: Your son is with us. Do you want him back?

Parent: Halo, who's speaking? What do you mean want him back?

Kidnapper: Don't shout, Shyamlal...it could harm you....we have your son with us.

Parent: Where have you taken him and what do you want from me?

Kidnapper: We have held your son captive and will release him only if you cough up rupees 1 million.

Parent: What do you mean, taken captive and who are you making such absurd demands?

Kidnapper: Look, Shyamlal, we have kidnapped your son...we know you have lots of money...we just want 1 million from you if you desire safe return of your son.

Parent: That's a very big amount...I am a poor man...I don't have so much money...you have certainly made a mistake by picking on my son.

Kidnapper: We know you very well, Shyamlal. Don't make excuses. I'll call you again sometime later. In the meantime arrange for money and do not try to contact police if you want to see your child in one piece.

Parent: Halo, please take pity on me...I am a poor betel shopkeeper. How can I give you so much money? I have never seen so much money in my life... please spare my son...he is a small boy. How can I procure so much money?

Kidnapper: Don't try to fool us...we know you have a prime piece of land that could fetch you several millions. We want just one million. If you care for your son, you will arrange for it and if you do not care, don't worry about your son...we'll parcel his body in a day or two.

Parent: No, please don't do that...I plead with you...we'll try to meet your demand...only don't harm the child and please give him something to eat.

Kidnapper: If you take care of our demand, we'll take care of your child...he will come to no harm...but don't try to act smart...we'll call you again.

Parent: Halo, please...just one request...it may not be possible for me to arrange so much money so quickly... please make it quarter of a million for now...

Kidnapper: Now, you're trying to play with us...it will have serious consequences for you.

Parent: Sir, I am doing nothing of the kind...as you have yourself said, I have a piece of land against which I'll try to get some money. It will take time to collect so much money...I have to look for a prospective buyer who must have ready cash to pay for...therefore I request you to please agree to a quarter of a million for now. I'll pay the remainder after getting the money...meanwhile, I request you to please release my son after taking the first instalment of a quarter of a million....

Kidnapper: We'll call you back after sometime by which time you should be in a position to deliver cash at a place we'll inform you about. Is that clear to you?

Parent: Thank you, sir, we'll try to deliver cash after hearing from you and please don't harm the child.

Kidnapper: Arrange for the money quickly...or else....

9) Two teachers meeting after a long time in an animated conversation.

Pragati Prasad: Halo, Dr. Jadav. Long time no see...where you had been all these years?

Dr. Jadav: Long time, no doubt...I was on deputation to Bangalore and to Pondicherry for a while.

Pragati Prasad: Bengaluru and Puducherry, if I may...

Dr. Jadav: ...Oh yes. I stand corrected...you still have it in you, Mr. Prasad–correcting people.

Pragati Prasad: Old habits die hard, Dr. Jadav...have you then settled back to Patna?

Dr. Jadav: Oh yes, there is nothing like your own home...your own society...your own backyard.

Pragati Prasad: Do you still hold these sentiments?

Dr. Jadav: Why not? How can one live without these sentiments?

Pragati Prasad: Well, the way this world is evolving...it's really difficult to answer that...

Dr. Jadav: Why, what's wrong with the world....?

Pragati Prasad: It has become far too fast for the likes of me. New ethos has replaced the old ones. I find myself at odd with things around me.

Dr. Jadav: It's all a matter of orientation, Mr. Prasad...after all there's no difference between me and you so far as the age is concerned...then why this difference in perception.

Pragati Prasad: Your exposure to the world outside may have helped you re-invent or re-adjust yourself to the fast changing world...but I have stayed put here....

Dr. Jadav: To an extent, yes...but the change has come about, good or bad; it has impacted all of us. We have become more dependent on machines and computers which is why we must, we have to bring about a change in our orientation. Else we will be left behind.

Pragati Prasad: Left behind what? Are we in a perpetual race to reach somewhere?

Dr. Jadav: The very survival itself is a race today.

Pragati Prasad: I fear I am not in this race for survival then.

Dr. Jadav: Well, you say so because you have nothing to bother about...your children have settled in life....

Pragati Prasad: What worries do you have on that count? Your children too have settled down well enough.

Dr. Jadav: Yes, but they have not yet got the green card they have been aspiring for.

Pragati Prasad: That means you have not imparted the lessons on importance of home, society and backyard to your children! As for aspiration, there's no end to what you can aspire for. Or may be, as I said, they are part of that incidence of race to reach somewhere.

Dr. Jadav: These sentiments suit us more because we have grown old and have withdrawn from the active world. It all boils down to the question of survival of the fittest in this world of globalised market.

Pragati Prasad: This credo of survival of the fittest has been applicable to every age...our times are no exception. What differentiates this age from the previous ones is that we have allowed ourselves to be mastered by tools rather than we mastering tools and in the process allowed ourselves to become robots...we have ceased to be humans...we have imbibed western culture...we have become far too liberalized today than is warranted...that is why all this trouble.

Dr. Jadav: Don't you think it has improved the quality of our life?

Pragati Prasad: Yes, it has and it is visible; but, it has also lacerated everything that we held dear and that perhaps is not visible to many...this is what is tearing us apart.

Dr. Jadav: Some compromises have to be made, Mr. Prasad...and let's not forget the kind of strides we have made...we have emerged as a power in the world.

Pragati Prasad: I forget nothing...but I am not sure if we are making right kind of compromises. Becoming power cannot be an end in itself. Russia was a power. It is no longer a power. America is a super power, but how long it can remain there?

Dr. Jadav: That's what the world is all about.

Pragati Prasad: The world is what we make of it...all right...see you again.

10) Mother and daughter in a shopping mall

Mother: Let's immediately buy our things and come out of it.

Daughter: Oh no, Mom...we must go around first.

Mother: Why go around when we know what we have to buy?

Daughter: We haven't simply come to buy things here. We could have done that in the colony itself.

Mother: Going around will take so much time.

Daughter: That's why we have come early so that we could go around and enjoy things.

Mother: Okay, let's go around and see things first.

Daughter: Oh Mom, let's go there and see what has brought so many people together.

Mother: It's so much crowded there....stay away from it....

Daughter: They have caught a fellow who was running away with the purse of a lady....

Mother: So these places are also not safe, you see.

Daughter: The fellow has been caught...which means the place is safe. Security is very tight here.

Mother: All right, let us not go there...and waste our time.

Daughter: Our counter is here....

Mother: Let's go in....

Salesman: Yes, ma'am...what should you like to see...?

Daughter: Jeans for me...the latest one....

Salesman: Please be seated here....

Mother: Don't select very expensive one.

Daughter: Branded ones cost more than the normal ones....

Mother: Must we buy the branded one only?

Daughter: In the mall you get only the branded one....

Salesman: Here they are...they are the latest ones...shipped in only this week.

Daughter: What's the cost of this one?

Salesman: Oh what a choice, ma'am! You have picked the best piece in the lot.

Mother: Okay, what is the cost of that?

Salesman: Very little, ma'am...they are on promotion sale...only rupees one thousand four hundred....

Mother: Only? So much for a pant?

Daughter: You say they are on promotion sale!

Salesman: Exactly, otherwise its original cost is rupees two thousand nine-hundred ninety-nine.

Mother: This is funny really. Instead of saying three thousand...it should not cost more than rupees four hundred....

Salesman: Oh ma'am, you are in a mall...stated price is the price at which we sell here. We've already slashed the price of all items...no scope for further lowering, please.

Daughter: Show me the pant again.

Mother: It's very costly, just forget it.

Daughter: But the quality is good...elsewhere you would not get it.

Mother: Are you satisfied?

Daughter: Yes, I know it's good.

Mother: All right, pack it.

Salesman: Thanks for your visit...please come again. Pay across that counter.

Daughter: Thank you, mom...you are so good.

Mother: Let's go now....

Daughter: Oh, there are so many other counters to visit.

Mother: I don't have so much cash....

Daughter: But we have the credit card, don't we?

Mother: Yes, but your papa will not approve of it....

Daughter: Never mind papa. He will not say anything. We'll buy him a T-Shirt and you must buy a suit for yourself.

Mother: Well, you aren't going to settle for anything less than that....

□

Personality Development & Interviews

Overall personality of a person can be divided into the following constituents:

a) Appearance: This includes the physical stature, dress, gait, style of entry, sitting posture and the manner of departure. It is not at all necessary that one should have a good look and should be gaudily dressed. It is also not necessary that one's complexion should be fair. All that is required is one should be properly dressed and the dress should match one's physical stature and physical appearance. One must have a proper dress sense.

b) Behaviour: This generally includes the expressions we make before the interview board. All the four or five members are observing you, your manner of speaking. Your overall conduct is under scrutiny. Your expressions could be divided into i) verbal and ii) non-verbal expressions also known as communication skill.

c) Thoughts: Your thoughts are what give you out. This aspect of your personality has two parts. They are i) knowledge of the subject under discussion and ii) your outlook, i.e. how you look at the issues under discussion and how to propose to achieve results.

d) Recreation: Recreational avenues are the areas where a person gets joy when free from all social obligations. This kind of personality test is more relevant for those interviewed for defence services.

All the above constituents are present in each individual, but the requirement is that of an admixture of correct proportion of a specific constituent. Indeed, the personality of an individual cannot be changed in one go, but it can definitely be managed by pursuing certain principles while going for interview; as, the board will dispose you off in just about 15 to 20 minutes. They have just that much time to assess you and your utility and you have just that much time to impress the board:

Preparation for an interview is an important ingredient and a quality preparation maximizes your prospects of success. The preparation should include how you talk, how you face the interviewer, how you dress and the most important of them all is to know what to carry on your person for the interview. The attempt should also be aimed at making best possible use of the time available. The following tips should help you in boldly facing in the interview:

Invite information: Carry the document, i.e. print out of the e-mail/letter by which you have been notified about the interview. If you got the interview call over phone, find out the name and designation of the person who called you as well as the person or persons you are supposed to meet. Do some research about the company and the position. Keep this information handy.

Keep a copy of your CV/Resume: Always carry a copy of an updated resume/CV. It does not help to assume that it is already available with them because you have been shortlisted. Carrying an updated resume to the interview saves a lot of hassles, e.g. rather than having to explain all your academic qualifications all over again, you can simply show the CV/resume to the interviewer. Also, it helps if you have to fill in additional details.

Pen and paper: Carry a small notepad and a pen. You may want to write down some points during your discussion.

Your work portfolio: If you are in a creative profile, presenting your portfolio is as important as the way you present yourself. Do not carry the entire catalogue of what you have done; only choose your best work. Also, upload your work and share the link for future reference. You must also carry specific information to support your past accomplishments, if any. Once you are through with your studies, prepare hard for the interview. Mock interviews are a great help. Equip yourself with general information so that you give an impression of an up-to-date person.

Eye contact: Body language in an interview is more important than the actual language you speak. Maintaining eye contact with the interviewer helps in conveying the body language as also it shows you are not being evasive. You are ready to meet the interviewer head on. This shows your confidence, also your desire to get the job. The important thing to remember is–major part of all communications is non-verbal.

Positive attitude and conduct: Do not speak in negative terms about your past employers. When asked about your own weaknesses, do not state it bluntly. If you are in a hurry and are impatient to achieve your goals, state it in an action oriented manner. Say you are an extremely result-oriented person. Therefore, you tend to get impatient at times at slow or tardy progress.

Adaptability and relatedness: It is essential to be a good listener in order to succeed. Listen and adapt and be sensitive to the style of the interviewer and pay attention to minute details such as interviewer's attire, general ambience of the office where you are seated. These observations will help you in tailoring your own presentation. You should always try to relate your answers to the requirements of the company and always focus on your achievements that are relevant to the position. That is why it is desirable to do some research work on the company before embarking on the interview itself. If the interviewer shares some information about the company, encourage the interviewer and try to ask questions about your own possible role in the company. It is very important for you to know what employers could possibly be looking for in a candidate. Academic qualifications are not everything. There are other benchmarks too. Flexibility and readiness are the most potent characteristics and all companies would look for them in a candidate. Besides, sincerity and candour take precedence over all other qualities in an interview. Therefore, you must be honest in presenting your credentials. Do not veer around remuneration on your own.

Client testimonials: In many sectors, especially where you deal with clients, testimonials or recommendation letters are essential as it certifies and thereby recommends you to the prospective potential recruiters. If you are just out of college, you can carry college awards, teachers' recommendations and reference letters, although never talk about this before you are asked for it.

But **the golden rule is** not to carry too much and make a fool of yourself in the first interview. Rather, speak smartly and be frank about the fact that you are a fresher (if you are a fresher), underlining your eagerness to learn. In addition to all this, do not forget to wear your smile and carry your confidence–these are the ingredients that your interviewer would be looking for in you and these would finally make you click in the interview.

One of the objectives of this book is to lay stress on personality development and to lead the candidate to an interview board with confidence. Some valuable tips on how to present before a board that is constituted to interview a candidate form part of it. Interviewers are entitled to ask any question, if only to fluster you; but if one is well prepared, there is no need to be nervous or panicky about it. They have all necessary details about the candidate (you) in front of them. Therefore, they already know you and you can expect to be flooded with questions about yourself, your outlook and your views on things that will give you out. Based on the data they have compiled on you, they already know about your strength and weaknesses, your managerial skill and your knowledge. What, however, remains to be evaluated are your personality and your convictions about your work and the assignments you have in your hand or are likely to have. In short, the interview is about 'you'. Therefore you must take care of some dos and don'ts. The foremost thing is – you must know what not to speak; or, rather where to stop. This is more important than knowing what to speak. For, once you have spoken out, you have given yourself out. So you must be discreet in opening your mouth. If you are not sure, you must shut up, or say you do not know. And when you speak, you must be logical, consistent and rational. It is better not to make sweeping and generalized statements like *this is not possible; this can never be done; this will never succeed* or *this can never be achieved* etc. This will show the negative aspect of your personality—that you have already formed an opinion and drawn your conclusions. Such rigid attitudes are frowned upon and must be shunned. You should be open to ideas and therefore should not be disturbed even if the board disagrees with your views. If you are confident about your answer, state your position politely but firmly without appearing to be argumentative. You should be positive in your outlook and your positivity should be visible to the board. In fact, you will be well advised to do a SWOT analysis on yourself before presenting yourself for interview. A SWOT analysis tells you about your strength, your weaknesses, opportunities available and lurking threats you must countenance with a fair degree of success. Given below are two exercises on interviews. While one of them will demonstrate the positive side of the candidate, the other will expose the negative side of the candidate. □

Mock interviews

Interview Number One:

Chairman of the board to the candidate: Please be seated, Mr. Bharat.

Bharat: Thank you, Sir.

Chairman: Looking at your credentials, I find you have done all your studies in Bihar.

Bharat: Yes, sir.

Chairman: But the trend has been to go to other states for higher studies...you seem to be an exception.

Bharat: It's true the trend is to go out...but I am no exception. There are many like me who pursue their studies right here in Bihar and I don't think they are disadvantaged for that.

Chairman: Then how do you explain this trend?

Bharat: Well, sir, I do not see any logical explanation for that.

Chairman: What was your reason for not going out of state?

Bharat: My reasons were simple. I wanted to stay close to my parents as far as possible. I needed my parents by my side for their love and guidance; and they needed me by their side for support.

Chairman: It is very nice to hear a youth say so when most of them today seem more concerned with their career.

Bharat: Thank you, sir...for me my parents are very important.

Chairman: And how about career? Is that not important?

Bharat: That's important, sir. That's why I am here.

Chairman: Good to hear that...but what if you are selected and asked to go places? Won't that disturb you and your parents?

Bharat: Sir, I had said I'll try to stay close to my parents as far as possible...but that does not mean I'll not move out at all.

Chairman: Okay, Bharat. Let's get down to business. Your academic achievements are excellent. You could easily have settled for lectureship here itself...why did you choose this oil exploration company that may force you to leave the national boundaries?

Bharat: The prospects of creating resource for the country have always fascinated me. The world today is faced with the problem of fuel shortage or nature sustaining resources.

Chairman: We can understand your engineering degree, but why did you have to do MBA? If engineer is what you wanted to become, why this urge to become manager?

Bharat: Sir, I believe that every individual is a manager in the real sense of the term. MBA readies me for the onerous task of scientifically managing the affairs of any organization. This is required in any kind of organization.

Member of the Board: How long do you think fuel can last? Should we not explore other avenues?

Bharat: One thing is sure–it cannot last till eternity. It is, therefore, imperative that we look for other avenues...and in fact, many alternatives are already being made use of.

Member: Is that enough?

Bharat: Not enough and we cannot sit back. While explorations must go on without interruption, it is equally important that we make cautious use of the known and available resources.

Member: Where should the exploration stop?

Bharat: Nowhere. It's a constant process, a never ending process.

Chairman: Don't you think this is a tiring process?

Bharat: I do not think so, sir. Just as life is a constant process of living, so is this exploration. This gives meaning and substance to our existence...if it were not for this, we would long have stagnated.

Chairman: What you do in your spare time?

Bharat: I assist my parents in the field.

Chairman: With you no longer around, will they not feel the pinch of your absence?

Bharat: Yes, sir, they will...but they will adjust because they are aware of the fact that I'll not remain with them all their life. I assist them in the field not because they need my help, but because I derive the joy of being with them. It's purely my benefit.

Chairman: All right, Mr. Bharat. Thanks for your candour and sincerity.

Bharat: Thank you, sir, it was my pleasure.

Interview Number Two:

Chairman of the board: Please step in.

Candidate: Sorry, sir.....got delayed because of traffic....

Chairman: Please sit down.

Candidate: Thank you, sir. (Pulls the chair, makes noise and sits down looking awkwardly around).

Chairman: What's your name? (Chairman asks somewhat disdainfully).

Candidate: Akela Chouhan...

Chairman: Rather an unusual name?

Candidate: Sorry, sir.....I keep telling my father that this was not a good name.

Chairman: So, you don't like your name?

Candidate: How can anyone like this kind of a name?

Chairman: But there must have been some reason why your father named you Akela!

Candidate: Yes, I was told I was the only son in our near relations....

Chairman: Is that not a valid reason then.... and should you not be proud of this fact?

Candidate: I had not thought of it in this light...but now that you say so, I am proud of it.

Chairman: Alright, Mr. Akela, why did you choose to apply for this job knowing the kind of risks involved?

Candidate: I was not very keen ...my father insisted that I apply for all jobs that are on offer....

Chairman: Does your father decide everything for you?

Candidate: Not everything, sir.

Chairman: If you are not keen, why did you apply for it? How can you do justice to your job if you are not interested in it?

Candidate: Getting job is important...and I can develop interest by and by.

Chairman: Do you think this is the right approach in a globalized environment?

Candidate is not sure of what to say...looks nervously around and stays put.

Co-chairman: Well, Mr. Akela...you have studied history and you appear to have done well in this paper...what interests you in history?

Candidate: Nothing in particular, sir. But I have special liking for Shivaji.

Co-chairman: Why so?

Candidate: Because he successfully challenged the power of Aurangzeb.

Co-chairman: Successfully? Do you mean to say Shivaji drove Aurangzeb out of India and ended the Mughal rule?

Candidate: Had he lived longer, he would have done that.
Chairman: Are you sure of your facts, Mr. Akela?
Candidate: Sir, these are not my facts...these are the facts of history.
Chairman: I see...you appear to be a serious student of history...all right, how do you see India ten years from hence?
Candidate: India is a super-power in the making.
Chairman: What makes you say so?
Candidate: It's not what I say...Dr. Kalam has said so....
Chairman: Thank you, Mr. Akela...enough for the day.
Candidate: Thank you, sir.

Both the interviews are important. They show the contrast so very clearly and effectively. Bharat in the first interview is sure of himself and of his situation. He not only sees positive in everything around him, but also demonstrates it with assurance and confidence. He not only cares for his parents, he also has concerns for his own career as also for nation's resources. He would be an asset to whatever department he joins. Employers always look for these traits in their employees. Bharat is a sure shot.

In contrast, the other candidate Akela is full of negatives. He does not take pride in his name which is his identity. He puts blame on his father for his name. Instead, of extolling the uniqueness of his name, he finds it obnoxious. But once the board chairman provides a possible explanation for his father opting for this name, he is happy and begins to take pride in his name. He is fickle-minded and lacks both knowledge and intelligence. He is not sure of his facts; yet, he goes on speaking almost to the extent of driving the board crazy. He does not understand the sarcasm of the board, nor does he take any hint of subtle displeasure shown by the board. Such a candidate would never pass muster. Stands rejected.

Both of these interviews are expected to arm the candidate with necessary inputs for facing interviews.

□

Writing Emails, Faxes and Memos (memoranda)

Emails, faxes (facsimile) and memos (memoranda) can be similar in style. Memos and emails between colleagues can be informal, but business faxes and emails, etc. may be either semi-formal or formal depending on the individual relationship and on what the message contains. It is also common for normal business letters to be sent as faxes.

There are some basic rules for writing faxes, memos and emails:

- Do not write Dear Sir/Madam/Mrs. Ghosh or use a particular pattern at the end. Simply sign your name.
- Be consistent in style. Do not fluctuate between formal and informal. Stick to one format.
- Appearance has importance. Remember to use paragraphs and proper sentences.
- Keep it short and to the point.
- Use the subject line to summarise the point of the message so that the reader is clear about the content.

To Mithali Jain
From Suniti Chauhan
Date 14 January 2009
Subject Proposed meeting tomorrow

Hi Mithali,
Matter of great pleasure to inform that I have obtained necessary permission to attend the proposed meeting scheduled for tomorrow. Rest assured, I shall be there right on time.
Suniti

To cmc@cmsindofine.com
From Pussycat.lycos.com
Date 14 January 2009
Subject Winter garments

Dear Samir,
The stock of garments has arrived just today; and we are now in a position to ship your consignment. We will highly appreciate if you advise us about your readiness to take expeditious delivery of the shipped goods.

Bimal Jalan
Manager
Pussycat Garments
Tel: 011-26844179
Fax: 011-26933961

Fax	Memo
Bhuvan Publishers, 46, Plaza Amba, Pusa Road, New Delhi-110005	Bhuvan Publishers,
Fax To Fr. D'Souza, Premier Books From BC Nigam Fax No 011 24472541 Subject Manuscript Date 22 January 2009 Pages including this 1	Memorandum To: All auditors From: N. Jayraman Subject: Sale proceeds Date: 26 March 2009

Refer to our telephonic talk of date. The relevant pages of the manuscript have been couriered to you for your final viewing. Please return the same after doing the needful. BC Nigam Project Manager	Sale proceeds for December together with audited receipts are attached. The Sale proceeds for December meeting is scheduled for 27.03.2009 at 1.30 p.m. in the Conference Hall. Jayraman

Electronic messaging

Writing of postcards for sending messages and sending of telegrams for cryptic but urgent missives are no longer in vogue; they have long been replaced by electronic messaging. Therefore, we must learn the rudiments of electronic messaging. Text messages, chat room messages and even emails can be written using possibly the smallest number of letters. Abbreviations can be widely used and pronouns, prepositions and articles can altogether be dispensed with. Given below are some of the examples of how words can be used in messages:

2DAY	today	L0L	lots of love/luck/laughing out loud
2MORO	tomorrow	MSG	message
2NITE	tonight	MYOB	mind your own business
ASAP	as soon as possible	AIB	all the best
B4	before	NO1	no one
B4N	bye for now	BBL	be back later
BTW	by the way	PCM	please call me
CUL8R	see you later	SOM1	someone
F2F	face to face	SPK	speak
FWIW	for what it's worth	THX	thanks
FYI	for your information	WAN2	want to
WKND	weekend	GR8	great
HAND	have a nice day	X	kiss
XLNT	excellent	XOXO	hugs and kisses

ILU	I love you	YR	your/you're
IMHO	in my humble opinion		
KIT	keep in touch		

You can express your feelings by using the following symbols that are called *emoticons* :

:-)	Happy (a 'smiley'J)
:-(	Unhappy L
;-)	Winking
:-D	Laughing
:-Q	I don't understand
:'-(	Crying
:-I	Bored
:-*	Kiss
:-O	Surprised
:-X	My lips are sealed (I won't tell anyone)

□

Advertisements

What is an advertisement?

Strictly speaking, advertisement is a public notice or announcement for advertising goods or services in newspapers, billboards or through radio broadcasts. We advertise because we wish to draw attention of consumers/prospective clients to goods, services and vacant positions on offer, and this is done through public medium. This is one of the most effective ways to sell/promote or to seek employees. We advertise because in this jungle of variegated products, we need to inform consumers about what is available in the market to meet their everyday changing demands. In this burgeoning market of consumerism, if we fail to communicate effectively with the prospective buyers of our goods, we shall be left behind and finally kicked out of the market. So, in order to sell products, in order to survive the cut throat competition and to sustain a business/economic activity, advertisement is a must tool. It not only keeps one in the mainstream, but also afloat. While this is the underlying principle and philosophy, the basic idea of advertisement is to reach out to people and to build clientele base.

There was a time when this was achieved through newspapers and radio broadcasts. But today the scenario has altered radically. While newspapers and radio broadcasts continue to play an important role to boost ad campaigns, there are many in-expensive and more innovative means of reaching out and for building clientele base. Electronic medium has come to acquire a very important place in advertisement. And electronic media is not restricted to television channels and visuals alone. It includes online internet facilities and all that goes with it including facebook, twitter and blog (web log). Net is the new radio. Web world has become an integral part of every individual who thinks global, not local, and has become integrated with every field of activities. Any activity, be it buying or selling something, can be done via a website. This shows that a website is like an online advertisement that helps in marketing a product or an idea to a number of people in just one go. So, an individual who is internet-savvy and can think out of the box can become a web designer and an effective advertiser. A web designer is an artist who decides and sculpts the look and feel of a website by employing his aesthetic sense and by turning a website into a product that sells. If we have one such designer in our midst, we have a classic advertiser in this web designer.

But there is no substitute for words. Words speak far more effectively than anything else. Visuals too cannot overshadow words. The only exception to this rule would be when the target group is illiterate. When the target group is not literate, visuals play their part though it is important for the visuals to relate to the product so that those who see the visual understand the relationship. Failure to relate with the product may be counterproductive.

Customer is the king is a maxim in the business world that stands out and is understood by all who are literate. Reaching out is the central theme of business ethics. The fundamental tenet of advertising is that it is the people who are at the centre of everything, and recognizing this is the essence of what a successful business enterprise does or should do. Gandhi's definition and description of a customer is an unassailable statement of fact which encompasses the spirit contained in the statement *customer is the king* in its entirety. Any advertiser will be well-advised to keep Gandhi mantra in mind while embarking on an ad campaign. Gandhi said:

"Customer is the most important visitor on our premises. He is not dependent on us. We are dependent on him. He is not an interruption on our work. He is the purpose of it. He is not an outsider to our business. He is a part of it. We are not doing a favour by serving him. He is doing a favour by giving us an

opportunity to do so."

Recognizing the potential advertising has, it is offered as a full-fledged course by many universities/institutions to groom professional advertisers. Ad campaign agencies and corporate houses now have media planning, coordination, R&D departments employing full time researchers. Good research is what contributes to making a campaign successful. Researchers find out what the consumer really needs, the craze, the trends of the time and design their ad materials accordingly. A good advertiser needs to inculcate the culture of innovation and passion. He must be ready to push the boundaries, or as they say, keep raising the bar. A world of advertisement is a world in a flux, and an advertiser has to constantly wade through it to bring out newer and attractive ideas/concepts. An advertiser has not only to think innovatively, but also globally because the ambit of the business has expanded beyond boundaries.

You happen to pass through a street where you see this ad atop a book stall: **It's raining books here**. You have not come out to buy a book. Yet, when you see this ad, you are drawn towards it and maybe you end up buying a book. This is the power of advertisement. If there are ads that draw you closer, there are ads that drive you mad and drive you away. These are usually the visual ads that you see on your television channels. There was this cement ad that showed a scantily dressed damsel emerging from the sea, and it is expected you will buy her cement. There are many visuals that will drive you away from the product. It's a bad ad. In order to market products with success, we must produce compelling product ideas that recognize what consumer really needs, make creative use of design and intuitive user interface.

Given below are some of the phrases or slogans that have the potential of turning into good and viable ad materials:

- We design it, you wear it.
- Promises don't take you places, we do.
- Laughter is a tranquilizer with no side effects–we provide it.
- We sell cubs, but don't deliver it in the tiger's den.

- Roses may have thorns for some, thorns have roses for me.
- We wrap you all up in yourself–our speciality; we don't overdress you.
- The price of success is much lower than the price of failure.
- If you have the passion for success, we have the means to ensure success.
- Vision is the art of seeing things invisible–we make you see them.
- Don't forget to live while striving to earn your living: we value your life and livelihood.
- We don't just make your dwelling house; we design your life in it.

These are some of the slogans that can add lustre to your ad material if you could fit them at appropriate places. Give it a try.

□

Telegrams

Telegram is the process of transferring long distance written messages through wireless services or such other services that do not require physical transport. Though telegrams are no longer in vogue (Australia has already closed this service in one of its major districts), this was one of the most effective and speedy means of communication till not in a very distant past. Since charges were levied on the basis of number of words, care was taken to write only what was absolutely necessary. Writing of telegram became a much sought after skill that not many possessed. Complete message in few or fewer words was or still is the essence of telegram. Since Morse code was used for communicating the message, the facility was available only with the telegraphic offices functional at district or sub-divisional headquarters. Morse code was replaced by telex, and telex by telephone at a later stage. Now telegram stands replaced by fax and emails.

Only the text of the telegram is transmitted together with the name of the recipient. Sender's name appears in the text itself. Some of the texts are given below:

Binay Jha
Station Road
Ghaziabad

Father serious Stop Come fast Stop

Alok

Sender's signature	Address: Alok Kumar Lanka, Varanasi

Rammohan Prasad
Nayatola
Bareilly

Matter settled Stop Arriving 14th instant with four Stop Make hotel arrangements Stop

Ranjit

Sender's signature	Address: Ranjit Tiwari Boring Road Patna

Parts containing signature and address are not meant to be the part of telegram. As you can see, in the first example number of words is ten and in the second example it is fifteen for which the charges are levied. Charges are uniform for 30 words and thereafter additional charges are levied for each word. There are only two categories of telegram these days: death telegram and express telegram. A nominal amount is charged for death message and it gets precedence over all other telegrams.

□

Precis Writing

Precise writing is précis writing. According to dictionary, the word 'précis' is 'a summary or abstract, esp. of a text or speech.' The essence is—be precise. Be brief and to the point. You come across a passage that has many things that are mere embellishments, at times supporting theme and at times just doing nothing. A précis writer has to weed out these linguistic embellishments that do not add anything to the central idea except lengthening it. As far as practicable, long phrases and idioms should be avoided. Adjectives could also be dispensed with unless absolutely necessary. There should not be any 'I' element. The narrative should be in third person.

The golden rule is: read the passage carefully and jot down the important points that need to be highlighted. Thereafter assimilate these points in your own language and give it a heading that should be sufficiently indicative of the central theme of the passage. Original texts must never be reproduced.

It is generally seen that a passage containing about 100 words can well be squeezed into a 25-30 words passage without taking anything away from the central theme. This kind of précis writing is necessary in offices where lengthy instructions, guidelines or circulars are required to be put up to higher officials/ministers for their information and for passing of necessary orders. This is required to be done in a manner so that the brief note put up to the authorities do not lose out on the essentials. In a précis, there is no room for verbosity. It must be shunned. Beyond this there is no similarity between précis and office notes.

Some of the exercises given below will show exactly how to go about it:

1. "There are scores of short lyrics, expressing the sentiment of love, tender, sometimes fanciful and sometimes full of unsatisfied craving, but always seeking for an ideal consummation of the sentiment. The different types and aspects of love Shelley ever contemplated are summed up in *Epi psychidion*. To analyse love that Shelley feels, one may say that it is a desire that always remains unsatisfied and that perhaps is never capable of being satisfied. He is in love with an ideal, and ceases to be an ideal as soon as it is realized. The note of yearning, coupled with the experience of a calmer happiness, untroubled by passion, which is so exquisitely expressed in the lyric addressed to Mrs. Jane William, marks his real attitude to love. In love he must find something ideal, something ever to aspire after, something ever to look forward to. It is in the non-realization, it is in the expectation of fulfilment that his happiness lies." (158 words)

Exercise worked out:

Love and Shelley

Constant search for an elusive ideal love is the essence of love poems. Pursuit of a never-to-be-fulfilled love enhances the prospects of happiness. Fulfilment of it could end this search and that could rob the poet of happiness. That is the essence of *Epi psychidion*, a lyric Shelley addressed to Mrs. Jane William. (52 words)

2. "The most obviously upsetting force to strike the family in the decades immediately ahead will be the impact of the new birth technology. The ability to pre-set the sex of one's baby, or even to 'programme' its IQ, looks and personality traits, must now be regarded as a real possibility. Embryo implants, babies grown *in vitro*, the ability to swallow a pill and guarantee oneself twins, tri plets or, even more, the ability to walk into a 'babytorium' and actually purchase embryos - all this reaches so far beyond any previous human experience that one needs to look at the future through the eyes of the poet or painter, rather than those of the sociologist

or conventional philosopher." (116 words)

Exercise worked out

Motherhood redefined

With facilities like embryo on sale and programmed IQ of the new born having become reality, motherhood is no longer the same. While social thinkers will be at a loss, it would take the imaginative powers of an artist to visualize the future. (42 words)

3. "Many books have been written about Joan of Arc, and in most of them the romantic and emotional side of her story has been stressed. It is indeed romantic, in the sense of being strange and exciting, and it does stir our emotions deeply to know that this peasant girl of seventeen put such pluck and pride into the faltering countrymen that, with her beside them, they succeeded in what they had thought impossible before. But that is not the whole story. Even Joan herself could not know the whole story. It did not end with her death, and its full consequences did not develop until long after." (109 words)

Exercise worked out

Joan of Arc

Much has been written about the romantic side of Joan's life. At the age of seventeen she led her demoralized countrymen to a victory that had looked impossible. But much of the real Joan unfolded after her death. (37 words)

4. "Amongst the many remains of the Harappa culture perhaps the most puzzling are the seals–small, flat, square or rectangular objects with a pictorial motif, human or animal, and an inscription. The latter remains undeciphered and holds promise of interesting information when it can be finally read. These seals, numbering about two thousand, appear to have been the tokens of the merchants, or possibly they were connected with the produce of the countryside which was brought into the cities.

Political continuity between the Harappa culture and the later Aryan culture was prevented by the intrusion of less civilized peoples who occupied the sites of the Indus valley in the first half of the second millennium B.C. By 1700 B.C. the Harappa culture had declined and the migration of the Indo-Aryans from Iran in about 1500 B.C. introduced new features into the cultural background." (142 words)

Exercise worked out

Unfolding of Harappa culture

Much of Harappa culture remains shrouded in the unexplored pages of history. Inscriptions on the large number of seals, when deci phered, may reveal some links about the people who occupied the Indus valley and the causes that led to the decline of Harappa culture and advent of the Aryans. (49 words)

5. "Indian polity has long been vitiated; it has been vitiated to such an extent that any thought or talk of its redemption could only be frowned upon. The decay has been systematic and a long drawn one. There is hardly any walk of life that can be said to be free from corruption or murky dealings. In fact, we have become so much inured to corruption and disorderliness that we now hardly care or bother. It has entered every pore of our system. We would not survive if by some strange method we should be rid of corruption and other evils that go with it.

Its phenomenal rise over the years has been unique. Not that it is unique only to India. There is hardly any part of the civilized of the world with very few exceptions that is free from this malaise. What however differentiates us from others is perhaps our near total indifference to it and to its presence in this measure; or, rather our total acceptance of it as a way of life. This indifference or acceptance is more damaging and disquieting than the disease itself. For, a disease can be cured if only there is a desire to cure it. It would seem that as a nation we have ceased to care for anything— much less the corruption and the related issues. When an ordinary law abiding citizen (perhaps he did not have the opportunity to break law or the prospects were not tempting or rewarding enough) notices the madness all around, he cannot help becoming a cynic. And once a cynic, you see nothing but dark spots. This is a frightening prospect indeed." (Words 274) (Excerpt from an article published in The Indian Nation, in 1995)

Exercise worked out

Corruption in India

Corruption has seeped into every pore of life and corroded the system. Even though corruption has impacted every part of the world, Indians have come to accept it as a necessary evil. There is a total indifference to any remedial talks. The attitude of accepting and being indifferent to corruption is disturbing. A disease can be tackled, because there is a desire to tackle it. Not corruption. A common man noticing corruption all around him without possibility of redemption could turn cynic and cynics see nothing but darkness. (86 words)

□

Circulars

Communications for implementation of various schemes, guidelines and orders at the grass-root level are sent by the headquarters/head-offices/corporate offices from time to time in a form and format that could be called circulars. Likewise, when government sends communication to many offices in one go, they are sent in the form of circulars/circular letters. These circulars/circular letters usually refer to certain changes brought about in schemes, rules and regulations etc. and seek their implementation by the offices down the line. The opening paragraph of a circular usually refers to any extant guidelines communicated earlier. Whenever Govt. of India sends communications to all ministries, they are called circulars.

The opening paragraph/s refer/s to the changes that have been brought about with reasons thereof and usually mention date from when such changes become operative.

The remaining paragraphs, if any, lay down the procedural aspects that are to be followed. A circular is addressed to all offices down the line or to some specific offices down the line depending on where it is to be implemented. It carries an identification number and; generally is issued in supersession to any previous order issued by the same authority.

Circulars are usually not very lengthy as they specify only those aspects that have been altered and need immediate attention of those responsible for implementation of the changed guidelines.

Some samples are given below:

Circular

No..... Govt. of India
Ministry of Food

From,
Chintamani Prasad
Joint Secretary, Govt. of India
To,
All provincial governments

New Delhi-02; 11.09.2010

Sub: Procurement of food grain

I am directed to inform that in view of the obtaining situation with regard to foodstock in the country, the Govt. of India has decided to procure food grains from the surplus provinces. Instructions with regard to quantum of food grains to be procured from each province and the price at which to be procured will be communicated soon.

Steps taken in this regard and progress report on the procurement may be sent to this ministry on weekly basis.

Yours faithfully,
Chintamani Prasad
Joint Secretary, Govt. of India

Public sector undertakings' circulars/circular letters are slightly different in form and structure as can be seen from the one given below:

Punjab National Bank
Operation, Payments & Settlement Division
Customer Care Centre
HO: New Delhi

21st April, 2008
OPSD Cir. No. 13/2008

ALL CIRCLE OFFICES

Reg: Customer Service-Complaints of 'misbehaviour with customers'.

In a highly vibrant market environment, today's customers

are demanding a lot. Consequently, extending good customer service is no longer merely a competitive advantage; rather, mandatory. Under these circumstances, being apathetic to customer needs or grievance is highly detrimental to the growth and progress of our bank.

Majority of complaints received from our dissatisfied customers points to attitudinal impropriety on the part of the staff members at various levels. Many of the complaints received at Head Office point out to the misbehaviour/rude/indifferent behaviour towards the customers. This is serious because any aggrieved customer is severe blow to the image of the bank and also hinders in increasing client base and in turn overall business and profitability. Leading service organizations believe that customer is always right; under any circumstances, the needs and wishes of the customers are to be met. In this context there is absolutely no scope for rude/indifferent/misbehavior with the customers.

Under no circumstances, tolerate misbehaviour of any degree by our staff members and take firm and swift action to curb this tendency.

Please take appropriate action for improvement in customer service and minimizing the complaints.

General Manager

As can be seen, there is a perceptible difference between a government circular and a PSU circular. While government circular is brief and laconic, PSU circular is long and explanatory. This difference may be attributed to the fact that while government has only to convey a direction, PSU has to give a direction with explanation/justification. The above circular is quoted verbatim. There is, therefore, no attempt to correct linguistic glitehes.

□

Paragraph writing

Paragraph writing is essentially an expansive writing. A subject or an idea is given and the writer is asked to expand it to a paragraph. If brevity is the soul of précis writing, verbosity, without its negative connotations, may be said to be the hallmark of paragraph writing. Paragraph writing is an art while précis writing is a science.

A paragraph consists of a series of sentences highlighting some facts and connected with one another in many ways by unity of purpose. The main fact thus visited, revisited, explained and illustrated is called the theme.

Unity is the necessary ingredient of paragraph writing. It means the paragraph must deal with one subject at a time. A single idea is the kernel of paragraph. Digressions and irrelevant matters are an anathema to paragraph writing. The unity of paragraph is determined and shaped by the theme by not allowing a paragraph to go beyond the scope of the theme. All sentences of a paragraph veer around the same idea and lead to the same idea. Just as in a complex sentence the principal clause holds sway over subordinate clauses, so also 'several sentences of which paragraph is composed are combined together in sense (though they are separated in construction), by words of reference, demonstrative phrases, collateral allusions, and the various other devices of sentence arrangement.'

Although no rules can be laid down about its length, the length of a paragraph, like that of a sentence, must be determined by the amount of matter to be put into it. The matter depends chiefly on the breadth of scope permitted by the theme. The judgement must, therefore, be left to the writer. It must however be said that a paragraph should neither be very long so that the reader loses any sense of unity in it, nor should it be too short to leave the reader puzzled or dissatisfied.

There is no definite place for the theme. It could occur anywhere in the paragraph: at the beginning; in the middle; or at the end. If it occurs in the beginning, there will be allusions to it in the middle or at the end. The idea will be visited and revisited. This will alert the reader to the possible theme. For majority of writers, beginning of the paragraph is the most natural and appropriate position for the theme. Being at the top, it easily draws the attention of the reader and prepares for what is to follow.

Essential features of a good paragraph can be summed up as under:

- It must have unity of purpose. All sentences in a paragraph must point to one main fact, idea or thought.
- It must have cohesiveness. The paragraph must bring out logical development of the topic, point to point. Illustrations or events that do not relate to the main topic must be avoided.
- It must lay emphasis where it is due. In order to draw the attention of the reader and to give proper impression, each sentence should be given adequate emphasis and importance. The key sentence of the paragraph should generally be the first sentence. Words should be chosen carefully so as to arouse the interest and curiosity of the reader. The arguments should be expanded on the strength of the opening sentence and the paragraph should be given a striking conclusion.
- Variety is the spice of life. Sentences too need to have varieties. If all sentences are of the same length, size and kind, the reader will find it monotonous and boring. An ideal paragraph should be an admixture of long and short sentences.

In order to write an effective paragraph, it is imperative that some thought should go into it before beginning the exercise. The writer should give it a ponderous moment or two, grasp the meaning and significance of the topic.

Once this is done, the writer should assimilate and arrange his ideas and jot down the important points in a logical sequence and develop them accordingly. Repetitions, digressions must be avoided and no irrelevant matter should be incorporated.

A paragraph should read like a complete and coherent piece of composition done in an engaging style.

Some samples:

1. If I were the prime minister of India

Prime minister is the executive head of our country. India is a vast country and the prime minister as the executive head of such a vast country has a huge responsibility cast upon him. It's a daunting task to govern a massive country like India. I have certain ideas about how the country should be seen by the people at large. Therefore, if I were to become the prime minister of India, I shall try to translate those ideas into reality. One thing that strikes me so strongly is the perception of India being a corrupt nation. We rank 87th in the list of 177 countries and I find it highly insulting for a nation of India's stature to rank that high on corruption. As prime minister I shall keep this very high on my priority list. As a first step, I will ratify all articles of The UN Convention against Corruption and not just two as at present. Another important point will be improving food storing capacity of the country so that food grains do not rot when there are so many hungry mouths to feed. My endeavour will also be to narrow the gap between haves and have-nots by recovering black money stashed away in foreign countries and by putting to use enormous wealth lying in our temples. Linking of rivers will also engage my attention as I believe it can solve the problem of flood and drought. As executive head of the country, it would be my concern to provide quality life to our people. To achieve that, we will have to have a policy on population. Present rate of growth is unacceptable to me because it tends to negate all positives of development and creates problems that we could do without. Another area of concern for me is that India is perceived by many as a soft target for international terrorist outfits. I will like to correct this perception. I understand doing all this will not be easy. But as I said, it's a daunting task to govern a massive state like India and I am prepared to undertake this daunting task.

2. They also serve who only stand and wait

There are people in this world who think that because they are up and doing, they alone are serving. This is not correct and calls for correction. Usually, those who are up and doing are visible because they see to it that they are visible. Consequently, their activities whether or not contributing to improving the society they inhabit get recorded. For instance, a corporator moves into the town with some sweepers in tow. On his orders, the roads are cleaned up and he gets applauded. Maybe the sweepers too get their dues. But how about the one who had been watching the accumulation of dirt and doing his own to keep it clean as much or he could? Knowing full well, it is not possible for him alone to keep the town clean, he religiously visits corporator's office and pleads with him to undertake this "operation clean". It is largely because of his regular incursions that the corporator was compelled to undertake this job. It was God's message to those with vision that just because they prayed and served, it did not mean those with no vision did not serve God. It is John Milton who penned this line in the famous sonnet *On His Blindness.*

Those who are active or up and doing should not be vain enough to think that they alone serve the cause of God. They also serve who only stand and wait.

3. Where there is a will there is a way

While it is true that evolutionary forces are at work at all times, it is equally true that nothing is uncaused. If you just keep sitting without having the desire to make things happen, you will just remain seated there. But if you have the will to do a thing, there is always a way. Manjhi was a poor farmer who wanted to go across to the adjoining village to sell his products and to buy things from market. But he had to traverse a long distance as entry to that village was blocked by a massive hill. If a road could be carved out of this, he thought, the distance will get reduced by over twenty miles. It will solve the problem of the entire village. Government had failed to respond to the prayer of the villagers. So, one fine morning, Manjhi set out with a task at hand. He confided to some who scoffed at the very idea. They called it madness. But Manjhi had decided to shovel his way through this rocky block. When people saw him making a dent, some helping hands came forward and in a few years' time, the hill gave way. Soon the government also came forward to extend help. Today there is a formal road linking adjoining villages. Manjhi was honoured by the chief minister of the state and the road was named after him. If only one has the will, ways can always be found as Manjhi found.

4. Necessity is the mother of all inventions

Man was not born with all the facilities as we find them. He had to begin from the scratch. Life was a constant struggle for him. It still is. Depending on what he needs for his survival and comfort, he invents and designs things. It is these constant searches for meeting his requirements that goaded him to invent or rather discover fire for the first time in the early days of civilization. When the lightning struck a forest, his flock of animals got burnt and got baked. This helped him learn to eat cooked food because he had had the taste of a burnt pig. The need to ferry across rivers made him invent and design boat which depending on necessity got modified from time to time. It is this necessity that impelled him to fly into the sky and then into the space. If there was no necessity, there would not have been so many things that we have today. True, necessity is the mother of all inventions.

5. No risk, no gain

Nothing is uncaused. Nothing would happen on its own, accidents excepted. In order that something happens, one has to take steps and taking steps involves risk. If you want to pluck and eat mango from a tree, you have to climb up the mango-laden tree. This means you are taking the risk of climbing up and this involves risk. Perhaps you are not trained for the job. You are doing it for the first time and you are not sure if you will be able to scale the height. But this is necessary in order that you get to the mangoes. Even if you choose to pluck by throwing stones, you run the risk of failing as also of being hit by that stone. But if you decide not to take the risk, you will go hungry. This you can ill-afford. You have no choice. If you want to enjoy the taste of ripe and juicy mango, you must take the risk of climbing up or of plucking them by bringing them down. If you take no risk, you make no gain.

6. Better late than never

Life is too precious to be lost in a hurry. But this is exactly what many of us are found doing today. Those in hurry tend to forget this rule of life that it is better to be late than never to be where they want to be. In our excessive zeal to speed up, we forget that there is not going to be another day if we perish today. We can see another day only if we survive this day. Speed for the sake of speed is not desirable and this often leads to consequences that are beyond our control. What happens is, instead of reaching the destination one moves into a world from where there is no return. This uncanny urge to reach fast and to leave everyone else behind is a disease that is best dispensed with. It is often seen that even if one reaches the destination much faster, all one can do there is to wait. It is not enough for you to be there on time. The other person you want to meet should also be in time. He may not jump the traffic signal to reach in time like you did. He may subscribe to the view that life is more important than reaching in time. This is not to suggest that one should not be punctual. But punctuality does not mean you should ignore the realities of life and take undue risks. What's the point if you could not reach there in one piece? This principle applies especially to those who are known for rash driving, or who do not care for safety norms. It is for them to know that it is always better to be late than never.

7. A friend in need is a friend indeed

This is one of the universal truths one should never lose sight of and should always believe in. Test of a friend is when you are in distress, when you are in trouble. You will have friends and relatives clinging to you when you are in good nick. They will readily celebrate your successes and be an integral part of it. They will readily attend to any call you make on them because they have the assurance of your magnanimity. You too will have the satisfaction of having got friends you can count on. But certainly you have not tested them. Real test will come when you are in distress, in an adverse situation. When you fail to provide them the joy you were able to do earlier, they will be put to real kest. Because of your adverse situation many of your friends will desert you and you will be left with only a few who will really care for you. In these moments of need they will stand by your side and then you will know who your real friends are. A friend is need is a friend indeed.

8. United we stand, divided we fall

This is an old adage that has not lost its relevance even today. Unity is our strength. Without unity we can achieve nothing. That is the precise reason why divisive forces are always at work, to keep people from getting united. So long as people remain divided, there is every possibility that those who have vested interests in anything will succeed in their mission. Conversely, if people remain united on an issue, the inimical forces are made to lick dust. You will have noticed the kind of result India achieved when it got united under Anna Hazare to launch a massive movement against corruption. Government tried to break the resolve of Anna, but failed because the whole of India seemed united on this issue. Government had to relent and accept the measures suggested for passing of a bill that, according to many, would go a long way in eradicating corruption from India. This is a classic example that proves the adage that united we stand, divided we fall.

9. You reap what you sow

If you sow a seed of shrub, you cannot reap mango. This means you get what you give, and maybe you get it in the same proportion that you give. This also means one should take responsibility for one's action. If you do a good turn to someone, you may get similar treatment in return. Likewise, if you do a bad turn to someone, be ready to receive the smack. There is no point in blaming others for wrongs done to you, for knowingly or unknowingly you too must have done some wrong somewhere. It is therefore important that one should always weigh pros and cons of what one does and what possible, negative or positive, impact it may have on other members of society. It would be preposterous to think that while we keep doing whatever serves our own interest, the society we live in will take it lying down. We should not complain if society retaliates and causes us harm. One should always be ready to reap what one sows.

10. It's never too late to learn

Dr. Radhakrishnan, the second President of India, did not miss out to read and learn even during his last few days of life. He had an insatiable hunger for learning. There are many people who pursue formal studies long after their retirement from public life because they believe it is never too late to learn. There are so many things to learn, so many books to read and so many problems to academically resolve. This keeps such people pegged to the learning process. A learning mind is a living mind and a living mind can do wonders. Age has nothing to do with learning. In your heyday you may not have been able to read and learn many things you actually wanted to read and learn. Your preoccupation with your profession or the need for providing financial support to your family and to yourself may not have given you enough time to pursue your educational interests. But after your retirement, you have the time to do what you had inclinations to do. If you have both time and inclination, age cannot dampen your spirit. There is nothing that can stop you from enriching your knowledge. For, it's never too late to learn.

□

Note Making

Note making is an integral part of office work. Movement of file from one official to another and then to the final authority necessitates note making.

Whenever a communication, a letter or a letter of complaint of some kind needing specific orders is received in an office, it is placed before the competent authority for perusal and disposal. If the competent authority has a secretariat of his own, the personal assistant (PA) or the secretary examines these letters and puts them up before the competent authority. The competent authority briefly glances through them and endorses to concerned departments/officials with specific instructions. He makes short orders as:

> 'Please put up' and signs off to some particular official.
>
> 'Please put up detailed note for orders' and may sign off to the department head.

These brief instructions are on those communications that are fresh and new. There may be communications/letters that allude to some issues already taken up earlier. While 'please put up' is a normal practice, there may be specific, though cryptic, observations as:

'Why no action so far?' Or, 'why matter not yet resolved?' Or, 'Please speak'; or, 'what the guideline says?'

When these communications/letters reach the concerned official, he rummages through all records/correspondences. He also rummages through various files and flags the relevant pages and marks them as A, B or C for easy reference and for facilitating easy leafing through by the competent authority. Once all records are before this official, he goes through all of them and makes a note:

- Noting should be brief.
- Noting should not be made on the original letter.
- A separate sheet should be attached/tagged.
- Language should be simple and easy to understand.
- No personal insinuations of any kind should form part of a noting.
- If there are more issues than one, noting should be made separately for each of them to obtain orders. If they are not made separately, they should at least be marked as i), ii) or iii) so that the authority knows exactly what orders are to be given and on what issues.
- Extant guidelines/rules under which a decision is to be taken should be mentioned and a copy of the guidelines/rules should be tagged for easy reference.
- Assistant/Junior official should put an initial on the bottom left side of the sheet as a token of having made the noting.
- Noting should be made in ink or should be typed out neatly.

Some of the routine notes/stock observations that are made on the files are as under:

- Assistant/Junior official should put an initial on the bottom left side of the sheet as a token of having made the noting
- Seen, thanks.
- Seen and returned.
- For information only.
- Submitted for perusal/information.
- Please acknowledge.
- Acknowledgement received.
- Needful be done.
- Needful is done.
- Draft reply put up for approval.
- Notes and orders at flag 'A' may be seen in this connection.
- Please see the preceding note dated.....
- The required information has been called for from the concerned department and will be put up on receiving

the same.

- A brief resume of the case is given (Pl. see flag 'B')
- Revised draft memorandum put up for approval please.
- Draft has been revised accordingly.
- The proposal is self-explanatory.
- No further action is prayed for.
- The concerned ministry may be consulted.
- The matter stands disposed; no further action required.
- We may expedite the matter.
- Return of file may please be expedited.
- Delay is regretted.
- Matter is under consideration.
- May be kept in abeyance till orders are received.
- We may await further communication from the corporate office.
- Immediate disposal of the file is required.
- We may ascertain the fact from the concerned office.
- Application may be rejected.
- Action may be taken as proposed.
- Formal approval is mandatory.
- Please put up a self-contained note.
- Please circulate and file.
- Office may note it carefully.
- Court ruling may be obtained/attached.
- Explanation may be called for.
- The bill is verified, is found in order; may be passed for payment.
- It would be necessary to fix responsibility before the amount is written off.
- Notices may be issued to the erring parties.
- We are not competent to this pass this order.
- Certified that the matter has been referred to the tribunal for disposal.

Here is a letter of complaint received at Local Head Office of SBI.

Vishishta Vidyarthi
191, Nai Sarak
Karol Bagh, New Delhi-110 005
14th August, 2010

To
The Chief General Manager
State Bank of India
Local Head Office
New Delhi

Sir,

Reg: Denial of Concessional Rate of Interest on Education Loan

This is to bring to your kind notice that the bank has denied me the concessional rate of interest that was promised at the time of opening my education loan account number 114860001217 with your Karol Bagh branch. The loan was taken in 2006 and during the moratorium period my father regularly serviced the interest. As per the promise made at the time of opening of the account, we were told that if we serviced the interest during the moratorium period, we would be entitled to concessional rate of interest, i.e. we have to pay 1 per cent less than the contracted rate.

But to our surprise, when we approached the branch and requested for the promised concessional rate of interest, the branch manager informed that we were not entitled to any relief since we had not paid interest every month without fail. Now this is a new thing. There was no such stipulation at the time of opening of the account. Now after I have completed the course, joined an international outfit and want to repay the loan by way of instalments, bank has put a spanner. Bank has gone back on its promise and amounts to deficiency in service which for a bank of this stature is surprising.

You are, therefore, requested to please intervene and issue suitable direction to the branch manager to give concessional rate of interest as promised at the time of opening of account. I would like to mention with all emphasis at my command that there was no stipulation about monthly payment. Interest was paid during the moratorium period on regular basis without following any monthly regime.

Thank you.

Yours faithfully,
Vishishta Vidyarthi

The dealing officer is asked to put up the matter to the Chief General Manager of the bank. This is how the matter is put up:

GM/CGM

Shri Vishishta Vidyarthi, enjoying education loan facility with our Karol Bagh branch, has sent in a letter vide dated 14.08.2010 in which he has submitted as under:

- that he along with his guardian took education loan in 2006 for Rs..... He claims to have been told of concessional rate of interest if the interest was serviced during moratorium period. This promise is in keeping with the bank guideline.
- that he has completed his course and is now working in an international outfit. He is keen to repay the loan.
- that when he claimed the concessional rate of interest from the branch, he was told he was not entitled to this relief as he had not serviced the interest every month.
- that he contests this contention of the bank and claims it's a new stipulation.
- detailed guidelines about education loan is given in circular no. 115/09 in which there is no mention of monthly serving of interest. It says, "if interest is serviced regularly during the moratorium period, concessional rate of 1 per cent will be allowed on the repayment...." (Please see flag).

In view of this, we may permit the branch to allow the concessional rate of interest.

Put up for orders.

Initials of the DO

The file goes to the General Manager who endorses the view of the DO and suggests that an explanation may be called from the branch manager of Karol Bagh branch on how he came to this conclusion that no concessional rate of interest was permissible in this case, as his act has shaken the confidence of the customer.

Initials of the GM

Yes, allowed.

Signature of the CGM

In this way, the matter gets resolved. This office will now send a letter to the branch in which the decision of the competent authority will be conveyed to the branch manager. The branch manager would be required to confirm having done the needful and also offer his explanation.

□

Auxiliaries

Auxiliaries are also known as **helping verbs**. Words such as *shall (will), be, might, would* help main verbs like *sit, stand* and *sing* form a verb phrase as she *will be sitting*, he *might stand* and they *would sing*. Auxiliaries are of two kinds: **primary auxiliaries** and **modal auxiliaries** as shown in the table below:

Primary Auxiliaries	Modal Auxiliaries
Comprising of	Can, may, shall, will, could, might, would, should, must, used to, dare, ought, need.
♦ Verb'to be'(am, is, are, was, were, isn't, being, been...) ♦ Have (have, has, had, haven't ....) ♦ Do (do, does, didn't .....)	Negatives as cannót, can't, may not,could not, couldn't, shall not, shan't, will not, won't, would not, wouldn't, must not, mustn't, used not to, dare not, daren't, ought not to, oughtn't to, Need not, needn't

Primary Auxiliaries: All the three auxiliaries as shown above can also be used as main verbs unlike most of the modal auxiliaries as can, may, shall:

- *Be* attentive.
- She *is* an actor.
- I *have* the authority.
- Krishna *does* not relent.

In the above examples, they do not perform the role of auxiliaries. It is only when they are used as helping verbs do they acquire the status of auxiliaries:

- Krishna *will be preparing* the document.
- The cook *is taking* rice.
- I *have completed* the work.
- She *does* not *want* to sing.

Doing and **done** are the forms of primary auxiliary, but they can be used only as main verbs and not as auxiliaries:

- She is *doing* the work assigned to her.
- I have *done* the calculation.
- The job will be *done*.

Verb 'to be' is used in continuous/progressive form to suggest the action is/was/will be happening.

- The bandits *are coming* (present continuous).
- It *was raining* (past continuous).
- They *will be attending* the class (future continuous).

It can be used in passive voice as well:

- The building *was* brought down.
- The ships *were* asked to leave.

Have/has/had is used in perfect verb forms to suggest completion of an action:

- You *have* completed your task.
- She *has* prevailed on her father.
- I *had* demonstrated this to him.

Do is used to make a command, a request or to make a statement more emphatic:

- *Do* sit down. I *do* need your presence here.
- She *did* play her part well.
- Please *do* show some urgency.

Also, to ask questions in simple present and simple past tense, to make negative statements/commands:

- Raja *did* not meet him. (Negative)
- *Did* Raja meet him? (Interrogatory)
- *Don't* sit here. (Negative command)

Just as in the case of modals, primary auxiliaries can be used in questions/negative statements and in contracted forms in informal writings and speeches:

- *Are* they going to the cinema?
- *Have* they decided to work overtime?
- She *has* not attended the class.
- He *is* not going to take part in this game.
- I've taken the time out.

Modal Auxiliaries

When we have to add special meaning to the main verb especially to indicate ability, futurity, permission and possibility, we use modal auxiliaries:

- You *eat* (main verb without any helping verb).
- You *will* eat (modal used for reference to future).
- You *can* eat (modal used for referring to the ability).
- You *may* eat (modal used for according permission).
- You *could* have eaten (model used for suggesting possibility of an action having been completed).

Dare is the only exception in this category. It takes 'd' to make a past reference:

- You *dared* not touch him.

It must however be remembered that *dared* is rarely used as auxiliary verb. Consequently, many would re-write the above sentence as: you did not *dare* to touch him. *Need* and *dare* are the only modals that can be used as main verbs:

- She *needs* some solace.
- She *dares* to challenge him openly.

Need and dare

Need and ***dare*** as auxiliary verbs are generally used either as negatives or as questions.

Negatives

- You *need* not fret and fume.
- She *need* not worry about the work.
- I *daren't* go there at night.
- Don't you *dare* do eat this pie.
- No one *dare* charge him. (not dares)

Questions,

- *Need* you worry about such a trifling matter?
- *Dare* he question you on this?

Can and **could** are used to refer to the ability to do something, to ask for permission or to refer to the possibilities:

Ability

- *Can* you perform this task in an hour's time?
- Though she was handicapped, she *could* complete it in time.
- *Could* you do this work when you have time?
- *Can* she go alone?

Permission

- *Can* I sit down please? (this is less formal than May I sit down please?)
- *Could* I please intervene?
- I wonder if I *could* intervene on her behalf.

It is important to mention that when *could* is used for seeking permission, it is not a past tense verb. *Could* is used in preference to *can* to make a present request as it is more polite and less demanding.

Possibility of something happening

- The collector *can* see you at 11.30 (there is a definite possibility of an appointment).
- The collector *could* see you at 11.30 (there is a hint of appointment being arranged).
- The meeting *can* be arranged (there is a distinct possibility of a meeting).
- The meeting *could* be arranged (hint of a possibility, but nothing definite here).

In the above examples *could* is used to express doubt. There is no change of tense here. *Could* also refers to a past possibility:

The collector could have seen you, but he did not. (There was a possibility which did not materialize).

Who could have invited him? (Seeking to know as to who could have performed this act.)

May and **might**

They are used:

To make a polite or formal request for permission

- *May* I take this flower?
- *Might* I drop you there?
- I wonder if I *might* give you a lift.

The use of *might* in place of *may* is less common. By using *might* the speaker shows he is being cautious and lacks in confidence. *May I take this flower* shows the speaker has more confidence than the one who says *might I drop you there* or *I wonder if I might give you a lift.* The last two show the tentativeness of the speaker.

To make a polite suggestion:

- She *may/might* meet you tomorrow at the station.
- *May/might* I take this packet from you?

To express a future or present possibility:

- She is not home. She *may/might* come tomorrow.
- I *may/might* give up smoking anytime now.

The element of uncertainty or tentativeness is to be seen in the use of *might* in all the above cases.

Shall and **Will**

Both *shall* and *will* can be used interchangeably even as some people like to follow the traditional grammar rule which says that in statements that refer to the future, *I* and *we* must be followed by *shall* and *you, he, she, it* and *they* must be followed by *will.* In present day English, however, we do not follow this strict regime. In spoken English, there is hardly any difference between *will* and *shall* as both of them have the same contracted form *'ll* that give us *I'll, You'll, She'll* and *We'll* etc.

Shall is used in asking questions involving *I* and *we* when speaker is making an offer, a suggestion or seeking advice:

- *Shall* I shut the gate?
- *Shall* we dine together?
- What *shall* we do today?
- What *shall* I bring for you?

Sometimes to emphasize that something will definitely happen because someone will ensure it happens.

- The Army *shall* bestow honorarium on you.
- He *shall* be there in time even if he were to run all the way.
- It *shall* be done come what may.

Sometimes speaker gives emphatic command insisting on completion of a work/task.

- You *shall* abide by the orders and complete the given assignment.
- All of you *shall* stay here till the work is complete.

Will is used to refer to something happening in the future.

- The war against terrorism *will* continue to engage the attention of the world.
- *Will* I get the job?
- When the corruption is eliminated from India, we *will* lead a cheerful life.

Will is used to express willingness or intention to do something:

- She *will* certainly come to your aid when in distress.
- Why not, I *will* always stand by you.

To invite or ask someone to do something:

- *Will* you give me your hand, please?
- He *will* be considerate to you, won't he?
- *Will* you keep quiet?

To say this and not that is capable of bringing about a desired result:

- This will help you recover fast, that one won't.
- This will melt easily, that one won't.

To say something that generally occurs:

- As usual, she *will* come late.
- Whenever these ladies meet, they *will* gossip for long hours.

Should is used to indicate that something is about to happen:

- The team *should* be here in an hour's time.
- The game is to start soon. The players *should* be moving in anytime now.

To suggest that the speaker believes that what is said is morally right and good for the person concerned:

- Children *should* abide by their guardians.
- Singers *should* be felicitated.
- Patients *should* be well looked after.
- You *should* be punctual in your class.

To ask someone for advice or instructions:

- What *should* I do now?
- *Should* I just stand at the gate?
- *Shouldn't* we bring in the guests?

To give advice, instructions or suggestions:

- Medicine *should* be taken regularly.
- They *shouldn't* work overtime.

Would is generally used to make a polite request:

- *Would* you do me a favour, please? '*Will* you do me a favour, please' will not sound polite enough.

  To offer something politely by way of question:

- *Would* you like to dance with me or *would* you like to spend some time with me?

A polite way of expressing want with the use of like.

- I *would* like to have a cup of tea with you, please.
- In all the above examples, *will* may not have the same appeal as *would*.

To refer to the result of a possible situation:

- Without internet, this computer *would* not serve any purpose.
- If you could arrange for a connection, I *would* be highly obliged to you.

In a conditional clause that refers to a highly improbable situation or to something that did not happen.

What *would* you do if you were not born to your parents?

Should and *would* are used as past tense in reported speech after a past reporting verb.

- 'Shall I do it?' He asked if he *should* do it.
- 'I'll do the job tomorrow.' He said that he *would* do the job the next day.

While referring to the future in the past, an allusion may be made to a past action that had not occurred at the time the speaker is alluding to:

- It was at Pune that he first encountered the lady whom he *would* eventually marry.

Or statements that simply refer to past habits:

- When we were small, we *would* make pranks every now and then.
- When they were young, they *would* go scouting every other day.

Must

Must is used to say something that is necessary or mandatory:

- Soldiers *must* put on their uniform.
- You *must* ensure that there is sufficient stock of food.

It is used for giving a firm order:

- We *must* do as we are told to do.

It is used to give advice or to make recommendations:

- We *must* obey the rules–it will give us peace of mind.
- We *must* watch this spectacle–it is worth watching.

It is used to state something that is likely to be true:

- She *must* be the one you are looking for. She matches the description.
- You took pains for her. You *must* be her well-wisher.

It is used to ask definitive questions as these:

- *Must* you torment me like this?
- *Must* I always follow you?
- *Must* it be reported to the principal?

The important thing to remember about *must* is that it refers only to present and future. For reference to the past, *had to* is to be used in place of *must*:

Direct speech '*I must go now*' will become '*He said that he had to go then*' as reported speech.

Ought to

This suggests that a particular action is the desirable thing to do:

- We *ought to* organize this meeting.
- You *ought to* accept your complicity.
- They *ought to* follow the rules.

This also suggests that something is more likely to happen because it appears to be more logical:

- The project started several months ago and so it *ought to* have been completed.
- We *ought to* have been ready by now, for this is the time for the show to start.

Even though *ought to* and *should* are interchangeable, *ought to* is less emphatic than *should*. Besides, *should* has other shades of meaning not synonymous with *ought to*. But both *ought to* and *should* are less emphatic than *must*:

- We *ought to* go now =We *should* go now (interchangeable).
- You *ought to* complete the job. (advice with no emphasis)
- You *should* complete the job. (advice with some emphasis)
- You *must* complete the job. (an order or a very strong advice)

Used to

This is used to refer to a past habit:

- He used to teach English, but he no longer seems interested in it.
- They used to visit this place every day when they were young and energetic.

As *used to* is in the past tense, it cannot refer to present or future activities. Its negative forms *used not to* and *did not use to* are not much in vogue:

- She used not to like mathematics when in school, but she excels in it now.
- He did not use to play chess in his schooling days, but is now a champion.

Questions with *used to* can be formed as shown below, but the usages are uncommon:

- *Used* she *to* study here?
- *Did* she *use to* study here?
- She *used to* study here, didn't she? □

Prefix

It consists of a syllable or two such as pre-, super-, un- that are added to the rootword and in the process add new or change its meaning:

Prefix	Root Word	Word formed
Pre- (meaning: before)	dominant	Predominant (being the strongest/main element)
Un- (meaning: not)	attractive	unattractive (not attractive)
Super- (meaning: above others)	structure	superstructure (a structure built on top of something)

Basic part of a word, also called stem, cannot stand on its own. It needs prefix. For instance, *couth, dict* and *fluous* are mere stems and they will need prefix to become words as: *uncouth, predict* and *superfluous.* As the word itself suggests, a prefix is that syllable which is put before a stem to form a word. Some of the key prefixes are given below with their meaning and examples:

Prefix	Meaning	Examples
a-	not	amoral, apolitical
a-	on	aboard, ashore, afloat
ab-, abs-	away, from	abnormal, abstinence, absent
ambi-	on both sides	ambivalent, ambidextrous
amphi-	around, on both sides	amphitheatre, amphibious
ante-	before	ante-room, antecedent
anti-	against	antithesis, antidote, antibiotic
auto-	self	autobiography, autograph

be-	to make	befriend, belittle
bi-	having two, twice	binary, bigamy, bilateral
bio-	life	biography, biology
circum-	around	circumference, circumlocution
co-	with	coeducation, cooperate
counter-	against	counterattack, countercharge
de-	away, down	debase, dethrone, debase, detach
demi-	half	demigod, demiofficial
dis-	apart, not	dissimilar, disagree, disown
ex-	formerly	ex-minister, ex-manager
ex-	out of	exclude, exhale, exhume, expatriate
fore-	before, in front of	forenoon, foremost, foretell
homo-	same	homogeneous, homosexual
hyper-	over	hypercritical, hypersensitive
il-	not	illegal, illicit, illiterate
im-	not	impartial, imperfect, impossible
in-	not	inaccurate, inaccessible, inconsiderate
in-	into	inject, inhale, inbred
inter-	between	intersession, intermission, interact
ir-	not	irregular, irrelevant
mal-	bad, ill	malfunction, malpractice
mis-	bad, wrong	misgovernance, misinformation
mono-	single, one	monosyllable, monoact
non-	not	nonconformist, nondescript
ob-	against	obfuscate, object, obstacle
off-	from	offset, offload, offspring
out-	beyond	outdo, outgrow, outsmart, outlive
over-	over	overestimate, overdraw, overdo
pan-	all	panorama, pan-America
poly-	many	polygamy, polygon
post-	after	post-war, postmortem, postpone
pre-	before	preview, prehistoric, prearranged
pro-	in support of	pro-reformist, pro-Islamic
pseudo-	false	pseudonym, pseudo-intellectual
re-	again	reappear, reemerge, recharge

semi-	half	semi-literate, semicolon, semi-final
sub-	under	sub-normal, sub-standard
super-	above, over	superfluous, supernatural
sym-	with	sympathy, symbiosis
syn-	with	synonym, synthesis
tele-	from afar or distance	telegram, telephone, telepathy
trans-	across, over	trans-continental, transnational
tri-	three	tricolor, tri partite, triumvirate
ultra-	beyond, very	ultramodern, ultrasound, ultraviolet
un-	not	unattractive, unlike, uncommon
un-	reverse	unburden, unforgiving, undo
uni-	one	unicorn, uniform, unison, unisex
vice-	the rank below	vice-captain, vice-chancellor
with	withdraw away, pull back	withdraw, withhold

While majority of prefixes are joined to root words without hyphenating them, there are some exceptions to this rule and such prefixes are *all-*, *self-*, *ex-* and they form words like *all-pervasive, all-embracing, all-encompassing; self-regulatory, self-disciplined, self-styled; ex-manager, ex-husband* and *ex-minister* etc..

There are some writers who put a hyphen between a prefix and a root word if the prefix ends and the root word begins with the same vowel. For instance, *co-operate, co-relate, re-enter, re-elect.* However, this practice is not followed by the present day writers and they prefer them as *cooperate, correlate, reenter* and *reelect.* But if there is a possibility of misunderstanding, the golden rule is to hyphenate them. While *resign* means *to give up one's employment*, *re-sign* means *to sign again.* Likewise, while *re-cover* means *to cover again*, *recover* means *to get well.* While *re-form* means *to form again*, *reform* means *to improve*; *re-creation* means *another creation*, *recreation means amusement; re-dress* means *to dress again*, but *redress* means *to make up for*. It is desirable to use hyphen between a prefix and a proper name: *pre-Raphaelite, anti-Israel, un-Islam, pro-Indian, post-Mouryans.*

□

Suffix

It consists of a syllable or two. It is placed at the end of a root word to form a full-fledged word. When *–ness* is added to *good*, we have new word *goodness*. Suffixes are of two kinds: *inflectional* and *derivational*.

Inflectional suffixes are i) added to nouns to form plurals and possessives as *cars, machines, Ram's, Barun's;* ii) added to verbs to indicate tense and number: *arrived, locked, changes, roads*; iii) added to adjectives to indicate degree: *quicker, quickest, dark, darkest.*

Derivational suffixes change a word from one part of speech to another in the manner suggested below:

- From assist (verb) to assistance (noun)
- From victim (noun) to victimize (verb)
- From beauty (noun) to beautiful (adjective)
- From good (adjective) to goodness (noun)
- From decorate (verb) to decorative (adjective)
- From fresh (adjective) to freshen (verb)

Derivational suffixes are used

To form **nouns from verbs**

a) –ment

Acknowledge	acknowledgement
Amend	amendment
Attach	attachment
Attain	attainment

Bewilder	bewilderment
Commit	commitment
Conceal	concealment
Disappoint	disappointment
Discourage	discouragement
Enforce	enforcement
Equip	equipment
Fulfil	fulfilment
Govern	government
Improve	improvement
Invest	investment
Judge	judgement
Measure	measurement
Nourish	nourishment
Punish	punishment
Resent	resentment
Settle	settlement

b) –al

Dispose	disposal
Renew	renewal
Withdraw	withdrawal
Survive	survival

c) –ure

Fix	fixture
Mix	mixture
Press	pressure

d) –t

Ascend	ascent
Descend	descent
Extend	extent
Lend	lent

e) –sion

Ascend	ascension
Corrode	corrosion
Descend	descension
Divide	division

	Provide	provision
f)	–ssion	
	Admit	admission
	Permit	permission
g)	–ance, -ence	
	Admit	admittance
	Acquaint	acquaintance
	Refer	reference
	Main	maintenance
	Confer	conference
h)	–tion	
	Appreciate	appreciation
	Depreciate	depreciation
	Complete	completion
	React	reaction
i)	–ation	
	Adapt	adaptation
	Adopt	adoption
	Condense	condensation
j)	–ition	
	Compete	competition
	Repeat	repetition
k)	–ification	
	Amplify	amplification
	Notify	notification
	Justify	justification
	Purify	purification
l)	–or	
	Administrate	administration
	Counsel	counselor
	Advise	advisor
	Survey	surveyor
m)	–er	
	Bank	banker
	Manage	manager

Build	builder
Spray	sprayer

Verbs from nouns

a) –ise/ize

Amortization	amortize
Harmony	harmonise/ze
Terror	terrorise/ze

b)

Active/activity	activate
Captive/captivity	captivate
Facility	facilitate
Felicity	felicitate

c) –ify

Beauty	beautify
Class	classify
Mystery	mystify
Person	personify

Adjectives from nouns

a) –al

Agriculture	agricultural
Ancestor	ancestral
Bride	bridal
Incident	incidental
Tradition	traditional
Universe	universal

b) –ial

President	presidential
Province	provincial
Adverb	adverbial
Provision	provisional

c) –ual

Intellect	intellectual
Spirit	spiritual

d) –y

Art	arty
Breeze	breezy

Chill	chilly
Fire	fiery
Frost	frosty
Patch	patchy
Smart	smarty
Shake	shaky

e) –ary

Discipline	disciplinary
Fragment	fragmentary
Legend	legendary
Moment	momentary
Vision	visionary

f) –ed

Hood	hooded
Point	pointed
Rag	ragged
Privilege	privileged
Talent	talented

g) –ly

Earth	earthly
Mother	motherly
Friend	friendly
Faith	faithful
Sincere	sincerely

h) –ar

Angle	angular
Circle	circular
Muscle	muscular
Triangle	triangular
Spectacle	spectacular
Title	titular

i) –ful, -less

Care	careful, careless
Cheer	cheerful, cheerless
Disdain	disdainful
Disgrace	disgraceful

Mercy	merciless, merciful
Fear	fearful, fearless
Grace	graceful, graceless
Resource	resourceful, resourceless
Use	useful, useless
Wind	windless

j) –ous

Adventure	adventurous
Ceremony	ceremonious
Fury	furious
Curio	curious
Danger	dangerous
Marvel	marvellous
Monster	monstrous
Disaster	disastrous
Nerve	nervous
Odour	odorous

k) –ic

Angel	angelic
Atmosphere	atmospheric
Economy	economic
Majesty	majestic
Organ	organic
Romance	romantic

l) –ish

Boy	boyish
Child	childish
Style	stylish

Nouns from adjectives

a) –ness

Good	goodness
Eager	eagerness
Selfish	selfishness
Coarse	coarseness
Fierce	fierceness
Heavy	heaviness

Happy	happiness
Ready	readiness
Serious	seriousness
Steady	steadiness
Swift	swiftness
Ugly	ugliness
Vague	vagueness
Vicious	viciousness
Weak	weakness

b) –ity

Arid	aridity
Acid	acidity
Captive	captivity
Grave	gravity
Extreme	extremity
Legal	legality
Secure	security
Sensitive	sensitivity
Visible	visibility

c) –ce

Abundant	abundance
Affluent	affluence
Convenient	convenience
Effulgent	effulgence
Evident	evidence
Intelligent	intelligence
Ignorant	ignorance
Prevalent	prevalence

Adjectives from verbs

a) –ive

Prevalent	prevalence
Communicate	communicative
Compete	competitive
Compare	comparative
Form	formative
Invent	inventive

Illustrate	illustrative
Permit	permissive
Repeat	repetitive
Respond	responsive
Submit	submissive

b) –able

Achieve	achievable
Attain	attainable
Beat	beatable
Drink	drinkable
Eat	eatable
Read	readable

c) –ant, -ent

Abound	abundant
Absorb	absorbent
Defy	defiant
Depend	dependent
Differ	different
Observe	observant
Please	pleasant
Suffice	sufficient
Vary	variant

Verbs from adjectives

a) en

Black	blacken
Beat	beaten
Dark	darken
Fast	fasten
Flat	flatten
Hard	harden
Moist	moisten
Sharp	sharpen
Quick	quicken

□

Letter Writing

Language, both written and spoken, is only a way of communicating or expressing thought. But thought itself is a complicated thing and the exercise of translating thought into language is not an easy process. In speech we can often use gestures and facial expressions to convey something written language may fail to convey. A frown, raising of an eyebrow, a wave of the hand are tools and real units or 'words' in spoken language. But in writing we have to search for the exact word, phrase, idiom or turn of expression that would exactly convey and represent the thought.

For writing general prose, not necessarily letters, there are three main ingredients: *narrative*, in which thought units record events in chronological orders–sentences, paragraphs; *logical*, in which reasoned arguments are recorded on the pattern of cause and effect; *descriptive*, in which the writer pictures qualities,as they suggest one by one, of the objects described.

But the letters we write fall in two categories: those addressed to relatives, friends and acquaintances and those written on official business. Of private letters there is very little to be said here as they are informal communications for which no rules can be laid down. But writing of business or official letters (also called formal letter) is different altogether. The writer of business or official letters has to follow certain conventions. These letters are usually addressed to a designated person in his/her official capacity. The top right hand side of the paper on which the letter is drafted/written has the address of the writer. Under the address the writer will write the date which can be written variously. As per the convention, it can be written as 14th November, 1988 or November 14 (or 14th) 1988, or 14/11/1988. These days due to American influence on the language, many choose to write 11/14/1988, i.e.month/date/year usually shown as mm/dd/year. Choice is best left to the writer.

When addressed to an official in his/her official capacity, then formal opening to a business/official letter is 'Dear Sir/Madam'. Official capacity means such designations as director, manager, secretary of a firm or a corporation, or the editor of a newspaper or an electronic media official. In every formal official communication the opening is 'Gentlemen' when no specific individual representative is mentioned. This is called salutation and it is followed by a comma (there is a growing tendency these days to dispense with the use of comma, it is left to the choice of writer), and the letter begins on the next line, inset from the margin as is done while writing a paragraph.

The simplest ending to this kind of letter is 'Yours faithfully', or less commonly used 'Yours truly' followed by a comma, and on the next line the signature of the writer just below 'Yours faithfully' or 'Yours truly'. If the signatory is writing this letter in official capacity, then the designation has to be mentioned and the signature must be put in the space between 'yours faithfully' or 'yours truly' and the designation. Sufficient space should be provided to facilitate signature with ease. This is the position of an official letter. But there are demi-official (DO letters) letters as well. Official letters have the tendency of getting lost or delayed because of the mix-up with routine official dak. To avoid such possibilities and to draw personal attention of a particular official on any particular matter, an official may choose to write a DO letter to his counterpart or to his superior or to a subordinate officer. High officials usually have letter pads that carry their name, designation and other details of office together with telephone numbers etc.

Such DO letters are addressed to an official by name as 'Dear Shri/Mr....' It ends with 'yours sincerely' on a personal note. This letter is opened by the individual official himself or by the staff of his/her secretariat. The name and complete address with designation of the addressee is given on the left bottom side of the letter head.

In addition to the above, letters are written for seeking employment, for redressal of grievances, to report lost and found cases and many others. Given below are some of the sample letters:

Personal letter

C. Venugopal
34, Nangloi Road
New Delhi
21.03.2009

Dear Morrison,

It's been a long time since we communicated. Your sudden departure from Delhi in 2004 made me lonely in this huge city.

Not much has changed here since you left. Hope you have settled in your country with your family. That explains your long silence. I am writing this letter not only to renew contact, but also to inform you that I am being deputed to your country for six months to execute an assignment there.

Without being excessively intrusive, I'll try to take advantage of your acquaintance with the place and people. Please write back, informing me whether you are there. I assure you, I'll not impinge on your privacy.

Sincerely,
G. Venugopal

To
Alwyn Morrison
43, Texado, United States of America

Official letter

Inter-Office

Life Insurance Corporation of India
Branch Office: Bhagalpur

Divisional Manager
Life Insurance Corporation of India

Fraser Road
Patna

27.10.2009

Sir,

Reg: Policy No. 66644125 favouring Shri Sunil Rastogi

With reference to the above policy, we have to submit as under: the policy under reference was issued in favour of Sh. Rastogi on 12.02.2008. The subject was insured for Rs. 1,00,000/- (rupees one lakh only) and the amount of premium was duly received by this office. From our record we find the policy was delivered to Sh. Rastogi by post.

We have now been informed by Sh. Rastogi that he has not received the policy certificate. In the meantime, it transpired that some Sh. Rastogi has secured loan against that policy. But this gentleman who presents himself as the insured says that he has not taken any loan. Since, he claims, he never got the policy he could not have discharged the policy. Strangely enough, the discharged policy that we have in our possession does not bear his signature.

You are requested to please advise as to how to resolve this issue. Sh. Rastogi is breathing down our neck and is creating scene almost every day unfailingly.

Yours faithfully,
Branch Manager

Letter of request for any specific purpose

Social Awareness Society of India
Bihar Chapter, Patna

22.04.2010

The Principal,
Veterinary College
Patna

Sir,

Subject: Request for use of space for public rally/meeting

We have been advised by our India Office to place on record our request for seeking to use the open ground of your college for a daylong meeting/rally on a date between 5th and 7th of May, 2010. The ground space will be utilized for spreading the message of seeking to eliminate corruption from our society. Speakers from various strata/disciplines are to address the gathering which would be in the range of 5000 to 6000. Specific date will be communicated on getting the final word any of these days.

A favourable decision for this social cause will be highly appreciated. Thank you.

Yours faithfully,
General Secretary

Copy: To the District Magistrate, Patna, for advance information and with a request for providing security for the visiting dignitaries on a date to be communicated soon in person.

General Secretary

Demi-official letter(DO letter)

Bhuban Shome
Vigilance Commissioner

Vigilance Commission
Esplanade, Kolkata
Telephone No:
Fax No.
Date:
Ref:

Dear Shri Bhadauria,

Reg: Action Taken Report on Case No. 36/09

My attention is drawn to this office letter No. 188/ATR/09 dated 23.01.09 advising, inter-alia, to submit Action Taken Report on Case No. 36/09. I am given to understand that your office is yet to take a view on the matter. Needless to say the delay has hampered compilation work in this office resulting in failure to timely submit the information to the ministry.

The case should ordinarily have been closed by now. By letting it prolong, your office gives an impression of being indifferent to matters of such importance. This attitude of indifference right under your nose is not appreciated.

I, therefore, call upon you to take immediate steps and get the case closed at the earliest. A confirmation to this effect together with ATR may be sent to me without any further loss of time.

With greetings,

Yours sincerely,
(Bhuban Shome)

Shri GS Bhadauria
General Manager
Steel Authority of India Limited
Kolkata

□□□